Following Christ

Following Christ

WALKING WITH JESUS
VOLUME FIVE

*An Expository Commentary
based upon Paul's Letter to the Ephesians*

(CHAPTER FOUR VERSES 17–32)

ROBERT B. CALLAHAN, SR.

RESOURCE *Publications* · Eugene, Oregon

FOLLOWING CHRIST
An Expository Commentary based upon Paul's Letter to the Ephesians
(Chapter 4 Verses 17–32)

Copyright © 2012 Robert B. Callahan, Sr. All rights reserved. Except for brief quotations in critical publications or reviews, no part of this book may be reproduced in any manner without prior written permission from the publisher. Write: Permissions, Wipf and Stock Publishers, 199 W. 8th Ave., Suite 3, Eugene, OR 97401.

Resource Publications
An Imprint of Wipf and Stock Publishers
199 W. 8th Ave., Suite 3
Eugene, OR 97401
www.wipfandstock.com

ISBN 13: 978-1-60899-649-0
Manufactured in the U.S.A.

All scripture quotations, unless otherwise indicated, are taken from the Holy Bible, The King James Study Bible, Copyright ©1983, 1988. (Previously published as the Liberty Annotated Study Bible and as The Annotated Study Bible, King James Version) Copyright © 1988 by Liberty University. Thomas Nelson Publishers.

*For my wife, Ginger,
whose encouragement, faith,
love, and objectivity contributed
significantly to Walking with Jesus*

Topical Categories in Walking with Jesus
(An Expository Commentary)

Volume One	Volume Two	Volume Three	Volume Four
The Triune God Speaks to the Saints	*Sin and Redemption*	*Christ's Prisoner*	*Walking As Mature Christians*
To the Faithful in Christ Jesus	Sin and God's Wrath	For This Cause—God's Glory	Living in Harmony With Christ
God's Will—Spiritual Blessings	God, Rich in Mercy and Grace	Revealing God's Hidden Truths	Unity in the Triune God The Holy Spirit
Trusting in Him	A Right Relationship With God	Praying to the Father	The Lord Jesus Christ
Praying for Christians	Reconciliation	Believing God's Power	God, the Father
	Praying Through the Holy Spirit		Grace According to Christ's Gifts
	God's Foundation (Apostles and Prophets)		Maturing in Christ

Topical Categories in Walking with Jesus
(An Expository Commentary)

Volume Five	Volume Six	Volume Seven	Volume Eight
Following Christ	*Walking Wisely*	*Satan and God's Armor*	*Christ's Ambassadors*
Alienated from God	Christ-Like Conduct	Family Relationships	A Call to Discipleship
Ye Have Not So Learned Christ	No Inheritance in the Kingdom of God and Christ	Life's Basic Relationship	Wearing God's Armor
Christ-Like Conduct	Walking in the Light	The Whole Armor of God	Christ's Ambassadors
	Walking Circumspectly	Satan and His Evil Forces	
	The Marriage Relationship		
	Christ and His Church		

Ephesians "brings one into an atmosphere of unbounded spiritual affluence that creates within one's heart deepest peace and assurance. It is impossible to live habitually in Ephesians and be depressed."

Ruth Paxson

Contents

Volume Five: Topical Categories xi
Foreword xiii
Preface xv
Acknowledgments xvii
The Question of Authorship xix
Introduction xxi

1 Walk Not as Other Gentiles 1

2 The Vanity (Futility) of Their Mind 11

3 Hardness of Their Hearts 21

4 Alienated from God 31

5 Contrasts: In Christ—Outside Christ 40

6 Knowing the Truth 50

7 God's Amazing Grace 58

8 Corrupt Through the Lusts of Deceit 68

9 The Power of God 76

10 Controlled by the Spirit of Christ 85

11 Created in Righteousness 93

12 Truth According to God 101

13 Speaking the Truth 111

14 Anger—Sinful or Righteous 120

15 Steal No More, Labor, and Give to the Needy 129

16 Communicating with Believers and Non-Believers 137

17 Grieve Not the Holy Spirit 148

18 A Walk in Love 156

Outline Questions 167
Bibliography 205
Scripture Index 207

Volume Five: Topical Categories

Category	Scripture	Chapters
Alienated From God	Eph. 4:17–19	1–4
Ye Have Not So Learned Christ	Eph 4:20–24	5–12
Christlike Conduct	Eph 4:25–32	13–18

Foreword

Robert Callahan's multi-volume work of Paul's Letter to the Ephesians is both a welcomed and long-overdue guide for Christian living today. The Apostle's sense of the eternity and greatness of God, his emphasis on the living reality and exaltation of Christ, his devotion to God's grace as an unearned gift of enduring love, and his call to an ardent and faithful discipleship all witness to an urgency and renewal critically needed in our time. Callahan's heart and style rise to meet this challenge and to convey God's message of hope and promise, of presence and courage, to Christian souls of any and every contemporary Christian tradition.

Callahan's format allows for both a devotional and studious usage. One can permit one's soul to savor every spiritual nuance the author uncovers, verse by verse, mark the passage, and return later for further nourishment. Or one can linger from text to text, gleaning with the author both theological and spiritual insight for enhancing personal discipleship, equally applicable in the arena of church and society.

The author draws on an array of insightful theological and spiritual wisdom, garnered from scholars and saints alike, theologians and missionaries. Calvin's Institutes guide Callahan's expositions, as well as the work of Markus Barth—known for his commentary on Ephesians and his delineation of Pauline theology. The author cites frequent and astute observations from Barth's exegesis of this nature. In addition, Callahan makes wise usage of Martyn Lloyd-Jones' emphasis on "experiencing the living Christ." For Lloyd-Jones, as well as the author, mere intellectual knowledge of the Christ fails to undergird one's faith or discipleship, when life's journey truly becomes sore bestead. Callahan also draws from the great 17th century theologian William Gurnall's delightful work: The Christian in Complete Armour. Perhaps students of Church history remember how both John Newton and Charles Spurgeon prized Gurnall's approach and piety and preferred it to many perspicacious studies available in their time. Gurnall's Complete Armour is known for its pithy, fervent, and wise counsel that confronts human vagaries with the truth about the self. In that respect, so too does Robert Callahan's gentle but firm counsel enrich the Christian heart and inspire one to a higher level of discipleship. No one can fail to sense this in Walking with Jesus. Whether encouraged to venture this methodology owing to his own years as a Presbyterian elder, or as an avid member and participant of the bi-annual Calvin's Colloquiums for the past 30 years, or as a fond reader of Ruth Paxson's The Wealth, Walk and Warfare of the Christian, the result is the same: a powerful, inspirational, and theologically heart-warming guide to discipleship today.

Ministers, Christian educators, seminary students, laypersons, and lovers of Jesus' life will find Callahan's work immensely valuable. His volumes deserve our grateful and sincere attention, as we too seek to walk with Jesus.

Benjamin W. Farley
Younts Professor Emeritus of Bible, Religion, and Philosophy
Erskine College, Due West, South Carolina

Preface

Paul's Epistle to the Ephesians shows us the joy and challenge of being united to Christ in his death and resurrection. It takes us from being seated with Him in the heavenlies (chapter 2), down to the battles we must wage, in His armor, with powers of evil (Eph. 6). In a balanced and judicious manner, longtime Presbyterian elder, Bob Callahan, exercises remarkable insight in opening to believers the vital truths of Ephesians; truths that once taken in, transform the attitude towards life, and often set the soul singing!

As a professor of theology, I have carefully worked through one of his multivolumed series, and found it to be theologically sound: evangelical and scholarly at the same time. It has spiritual depth and is extremely practical; it is accessible in good, clear English. It is neither a commentary, nor a series of sermons. In some ways it reminds me of some of the ancient Patristic engagements with a series of texts of Holy Scripture. It brings the reader into the presence of the Most High, and—if considered thoughtfully and prayerfully, is likely to cause him to sit down under the canopy of God's love.

The journey of Christians in today's world is very demanding indeed, and Bob's work is intended to be a guide to help every pilgrim 'Walking with Jesus.' It will be a rich resource for Sunday Schools, Bible studies, as well as for individual devotions.

Douglas F. Kelly
Reformed Theological Seminary
Charlotte, NC

Acknowledgments

The crafting of Walking with Jesus was not a "one man show" but numerous people working together to present a formidable work. Three guiding lights have been paramount in the minds of those making significant contributions: one, presenting the theology in accord with the tenets of the Reformed Faith; two, employing language that presents the Gospel in a meaningful and understandable light; and, three, expounding upon Scripture in a clear, concise, and forthright manner.

It has been God's blessing that the following ministers and theologians have enthusiastically and willingly provided their time and talents to enhance this work. They are:

Dr. Frank Barker, Founder and Pastor Emeritus of the Briarwood Presbyterian Church, Birmingham, AL

Dr. Benjamin W. Farley, Younts Professor Emeritus, Bible, Religion, and Philosophy, Erskine College, Due West, SC

Dr. James C. Goodloe, IV, Executive Director, Foundation for Reformed Theology, Richmond, VA

Dr. Todd Jones, Senior Minister, First Presbyterian Church, Nashville, TN

Dr. Douglas Kelly, Richard Jordan, Professor of Theology, Reformed Theological Seminary, Charlotte, NC

Dr. Norman McCrummen, Senior Pastor, Spring Hill Presbyterian Church, Mobile, AL

Dr. Mark Mueller, Senior Pastor, First Presbyterian Church, Huntsville, AL

Dr. Richard Ray, Former Managing Director of John Knox Press, Montreat, NC

Without the knowledge, wisdom, and encouragement of these individuals this work would neither have become a reality nor available to individuals seeking a better understanding of the teachings of the Scripture and the joy of walking daily with the Lord Jesus.

Several others have labored diligently to create this work, and to produce the finished product. Our daughter, Karen Callahan Myrick, made significant contributions during the drafting process through her knowledge of grammar. Ms. Lynn Sledge, as the copy editor, judiciously reviewed the manuscript and made valuable contributions for improving it. Four ladies, Helen Marshall, D'Anne Dendy, Kelly Comferford, and Elizabeth Annan, worked tirelessly, with dedication, to prepare draft after draft and to make positive contributions to the project. In addition, Wick Skinner made invaluable contributions through his attention to details, grammar, and vocabulary.

It is not possible to thank them sufficiently for their dedication to making this volume a desirable repository of Christian truths, and in so doing to cheerfully work on draft after draft, to recommend enhancements, and to make appropriate changes in the text. Their unselfish contributions are too many to enumerate. May God bless them.

The Question of Authorship

Recent scholars have questioned the authorship of the letter to the Ephesians and have been less convinced that it was the Apostle Paul. However, for the sake of simplicity of expression we will abide by the traditional view and refer to Paul as its author.

Introduction

The creation of this work was the result of unusual developments which some would attribute to happenstance and others to God's providence. You may be the judge after considering the following.

During May 2000 a friend invited my wife and me to visit the Spring Hill Presbyterian Church in Mobile and hear their new minister, Norman McCrummen. We accepted his invitation.

The following March, Dr. McCrummen was preaching on anything but Ephesians when he interrupted his sermon, paused long enough to slowly scan the congregation twice, and said, "I want everyone to read the first and second chapters of Ephesians by next Sunday" and promptly returned to his sermon. The next day I called him and said, "I can't do it" a few times. Finally, his light went on and he said, "What can't you do?" I said, "I can't read the first and second chapters of Ephesians by next Sunday." He asked, "Why can't you? It will only take ten to fifteen minutes." I responded, "I have fifty-eight to sixty expository messages on the first two chapters of Ephesians that took thirty to thirty-five minutes to present." His response was, "I want to read all those and everything else you have on Ephesians." Thus began the long, arduous, and heartwarming journey of converting handwritten notes along with printed ones into the written word. It has been a joyful, though demanding experience.

Paul's Letter to the Ephesians has been described as "The holiest of the holies." My love affair with it began in the 1980's when I read a book containing great sermons of the twentieth century. The most impressive one was written by Martyn Lloyd-Jones. As a result, I read other works of his including his exposition of Ephesians. Thereafter, unexpectedly, I was asked to teach an adult Bible Study Group. They said they would provide the material, but I demurred and said, "I would gather my own material." This set in motion the process of acquiring knowledge through the best expository works available at the time on Ephesians including Martyn

Lloyd-Jones, William Gurnall, Ruth Paxson, Markus Barth, John Calvin, Otto Weber, and others.

The objective was to present the essence of Paul's letter as it was presented to him by the Lord Jesus and the Holy Spirit. Further, to mine the gold available in the fruitful works of those fertile minds that God had cultivated and enabled to expound upon the truths that His only begotten Son had revealed to His apostles and disciples. Therefore, it was a paramount obligation to express God's truths in a simple, straightforward manner according to the dictates of the Holy Spirit so that the reader may grasp it and interpret it according to the will of our Lord and Saviour Jesus Christ.

The need for the truths of the Gospel is as great today as it was in the first century. The conditions are similar and the challenges facing our culture reveal the need for knowing the living God and His Son. Today, the people of faith require the same spiritual nourishment as those brave souls of the early days after the Resurrection, who would rather face death than deny their Lord and Saviour.

There are people in responsible positions in Christ's church who deny Him by: their passivity; seeking secular acceptance; and failing to honor Him in public. These apostasies negatively impact members of organized Christian churches as well as non-believers.

They create an environment in which unrighteousness flourishes. This results in irreverence as aptly described by R.W. Dale, "Where there is irreverence for the divine law the vision of God becomes fainter; as the vision of God becomes fainter the restraints of the Divine Righteousness are lessened and at last the vision of God is lost altogether." May God enlighten us regarding His infallible Word so that we will hunger and thirst for righteousness, and for the vision of God to shine brighter and brighter as we serve Him with courage, wisdom, justice, and self-control.

This expository commentary is designed to bring individuals, whether they are spiritually children, adolescents or adults into a closer, more mature relationship with the Lord Jesus Christ. It begins with the Triune God; presents the doctrines of the Christian faith; reminds us "that we henceforth be no more children, tossed to and fro . . . but speaking the truth in love, may grow up into Him in all things, . . . even Christ." It continues by emphasizing the importance of being renewed in the spirit of your mind; putting on the new man, which after God is created in righteousness and true holiness; using the whole armor of God to thwart the manifold attacks of Satan; and concluding with the admonition to conduct ourselves as Christ's ambassadors.

The spiritual food contained ranges from milk and honey to tough meat. The flavor of this exposition encompasses all varieties—sweet, sour, pleasant, bitter, tart, tasteless, dry, burned, and succulent. Do not reject the nourishment because of its texture or flavor, but seek to understand it despite your preferences, since it provides food for good health and strength for joyful living. May God's truths flourish in your heart and mind, and enable you to withstand the tests, trials, and tribulations that come your way as you are "Walking with Jesus."

In presenting this work, I realize everyone has different challenges. The fascinating part of God's Word is that it meets us where we are. The question is, will we meet Him there, hear what He has to say, and accept the nourishment He offers?

The words of William Gurnall are appropriate and enlightening in contemplating God's Word. He said prior to expounding upon Ephesians, "The fare that I shall be serving during the coming weeks will be from God's own table. If perchance it does not go down well or should not have the flavor that you desire, please do not despise the provider of the food, but blame the cook who has prepared it and is serving it." To that I say, Amen!

The courses being served by this cook are described herein. May they provide the taste and nourishment you are seeking.

Robert B. Callahan, Sr.

1

Walk Not as Other Gentiles

> *This I say therefore, and testify in the Lord, that ye henceforth walk not as other Gentiles walk, in the vanity* (futility) *of their mind,*
> *Having the understanding darkened, being alienated from the life of God through* (because of) *the ignorance that is in them, because of the blindness* (hardening) *of their heart:*
> *Who being past feeling have given themselves over unto lasciviousness* (licentiousness), *to work all uncleanness with greediness* [Eph. 4:17–19].

The first sixteen verses of Chapter 4 in Ephesians stress the unity, which is found only in Christ, and the church which is the body of Christ. As members of the body of Christ we are to study and practice His teachings. We are to grow and develop. We are to walk with our Master seven days a week. We are to be rooted in Christ. We are not to be tossed about by every wind of doctrine, the sleight of men, or their cunning craftiness.

In the last chapter, we considered five essential points while concluding our examination of Chapter 4, verses 1–16. They are:

- believing in the Lord Jesus Christ, the center of our faith, who is to be preached and taught as the only begotten (unique) Son of God;
- having a right relationship with our Lord and being in union with Him;
- having the life of the Spirit within which comes from Christ;
- examining ourselves in the light of the Gospel, praying for renewal and the strength to obey His commands; and
- responding to His call by increasing in faith and knowledge, and submitting ourselves to the will of God.

The Apostle devotes the remaining two and one-half chapters to applying doctrine and to practicing Christ's teachings. He devotes the following passages to what we are to be and what we are not to be. Some time ago, I had the pleasure of listening to tapes by Chuck Swindoll. One of the sermons contained a statement that is applicable to our study. He said, "I am not as interested in getting through Jude as I am interested in Jude getting through us." Thank goodness our concern is for Ephesians to get through to us and not getting through Paul's letter.

Paul begins the last half of Chapter 4 with the thought, *This I say therefore, and testify in the Lord, that ye henceforth walk not as other Gentiles walk, in the vanity* (futility) *of their mind*. The first characteristic of our walk with Christ is unity. It was examined in verses 1–16 of this chapter. Now it is time to consider the second characteristic, holiness. This is the essence of verses 17–30.

Paul introduces these truths with firmness and a tone of urgency. His introductory statement could be interpreted, "I *solemnly* adjure you as in God's presence." Paul transmits the burden upon his heart as he writes to them about the importance and necessity of changing their mode of living. He knew he was going to speak frankly and faithfully to them. Therefore, he wanted them to know that he was not merely stating his personal convictions concerning their life in Christ, but that it is the living Lord who is speaking through him.

Once again, we cannot overlook the word *therefore*. It is the dividing line between the heavenly calling in chapters 1–3 and the practical application in chapters 4–6. Paul was noting the fact that the Ephesians had moved from their old position in sin to their new position in Christ. What did this mean? The new position required a clean break with everything pertaining to their old ways. The new position in Christ calls for new practices. Paul calls them to an altogether different walk from those who are outside Christ. He says to them at this juncture, *This I say therefore, and testify in the Lord, that ye henceforth walk not as other Gentiles walk, in the vanity* (futility) *of their mind*.

The Apostle uses the term *henceforth* in this verse. It is worthwhile recalling what Paul said earlier, before proceeding.

Walk Not as Other Gentiles

> *Wherefore remember, that ye being in time past Gentiles in the flesh, who are called Uncircumcision by that which is called the Circumcision in the flesh made by hands;*
>
> *That at that time ye were without Christ, being aliens from the commonwealth of Israel, and strangers from the covenants of promise, having no hope, and without God in the world:*
>
> *But now in Christ Jesus ye who sometimes* (once) *were far off are made nigh by the blood of Christ* [Eph. 2:11–13].

You will note several things:

- *. . . ye being in time past Gentiles in the flesh, . . .*
- *That at that time ye were without Christ, being aliens . . . and strangers . . . having no hope, and without God in the world:*
- *But now in Christ Jesus ye who sometimes* (once) *were far off are made nigh by the blood of Christ* [Selections from Eph. 2:11–13].

In this thirteenth verse the Greek word for *sometimes* is *pote*. The correct interpretation of this word is "once" or "at sometime or other." Therefore, this verse should read, "*But now in Christ Jesus ye who* 'once' or 'at sometime or other' *were far off are made nigh by the blood of Christ.*"

By understanding where the Ephesian believers had been enables us to better understand where Paul wants them to be in their relationship with Christ and how they (we) are to conduct themselves as His followers. Consequently, Paul forcefully injects the thought with the word *henceforth* that "once" or "at one time or another" you were not in Christ, but now you are. Once you were dead, now you are alive. Something amazing had happened. The sinner had become a saint. How? By the *blood* of Christ.

Henceforth, life could never be as it was before. Since it could not be, Paul beseeches them to walk in the newness of life. Therefore, in the following verses he describes what they are to be and not to be.

Paul immediately proceeds to tell them what they are not to do, saying,

- *that ye henceforth walk not as other Gentiles . . . in the vanity* (futility) *of their mind,*
- *Having the understanding darkened, being alienated from the life of God, through* (because of) *the ignorance that is in them,*
- *because of the blindness* (hardening) *of their heart*
  [Selections from Eph. 4:17–18].

As usual Paul is direct. He does not mince words; he is forceful. He is not speaking with license, but responsibly. Paul wants us to realize that when we are in Christ we are entirely new creatures.

Before proceeding, recall the approach Paul has taken in writing this letter as enunciated by Martyn Lloyd-Jones, "In the first three chapters, the apostle lays down the Doctrine of Salvation; in Chapter 4, verses one through sixteen, he presents the Doctrine of the Church and what brings us into the church; and from Chapter Four, verse seventeen through the rest of the letter, is the outworking of doctrine in our daily lives, contacts, experiences, and conduct." The Apostle presents detailed explanations in each section expounding upon God's Word.

As we proceed to study the remainder of this magnificent letter, there are certain points to consider in order to better understand what follows. First, the Apostle never leaves anything to chance. To say the least, Paul is a careful teacher. He is never content to just enunciate principles. He never stops there. He invariably applies his teaching. The Word is always to be applied. We are to become knowledgeable as to how the Word is applied by Paul, Peter, John and the others through whom God spoke. We are to face up to every single detail and its application.

The Christian life is a life to be lived, and it is to be lived in particular details. It is not a philosophy. If we are not endeavoring to live this life to which we have been called in detail, then we are denying the very truth we claim to believe. This cannot be stated too strongly or too frequently. What did our Lord say?

> *If ye know these things, happy are ye if ye do them*
> [John 13:17].
>
> *For whosoever hath, to him shall be given, and he shall have more abundance: but whosoever hath not, from him shall be taken away even that he hath* [Matt. 13:12].
>
> *For unto every one that hath* (more) *shall be given, and he shall have abundance: but from him that hath not shall be taken away even that which he hath* [Matt. 25:29].

We have a great responsibility to know the truth and to apply it. We are to know the details, not just the generalities; the application includes the details.

Second, the life of the church and the life in the church are not to be a detached kind of life. It is not like a coat or dress that we *put on* and take off. It is like our skin, which is with us all the time. It is either clean or dirty. There is not to be a gap between our life in the church and our life outside the church. We all know instances where people are one way in church, or on Sunday, and another way during the week, or in secular affairs. Then the people outside the church say look at them on Sunday, then look at them on Monday, Tuesday, and Wednesday. When that happens the people outside the church have a valid criticism. The life of the person *in Christ* is to exhibit the characteristics of the Master. He or she is to strive to obey His commands and to walk according to His teachings each and every day. A person's daily walk in the secular world is more than having perfect attendance fifty-two weeks per year. Remember, the Holy Spirit is there day in and day out to enlighten, guide, protect, and strengthen His chosen ones. We are to acknowledge this fact by embracing Him, praising Him, and pleasing Him, by boldly and confidently serving Him all the days He gives us.

One of the striking things about Scripture is the contrast that is presented for our edification and upbuilding. There is a significant contrast in this letter. In the early portion, Paul describes the followers in Ephesus as

> . . . *saints . . . the faithful in Christ Jesus:*. . .
> . . . *the household of God;* . . . *built upon the foundation of the apostles and prophets,* . . .
> and . . . *a habitation* (dwelling place) *of God through the Spirit*
> [Selections from Eph. 1:1, 2:19–20, 22].

Paul speaks to them concerning the eternal truths of God and their perfect union with God in Christ.

Now he speaks to them forthrightly and warns them against the most base and demeaning vices. The question is: is he writing to the same people? Yes, it is clear that "These precepts, which imply not only the possibility, but the existence of such gross immoralities in the character and the conduct of those to whom they were addressed, were meant for the very same persons that Paul had described as 'saints' and 'the faithful in Christ Jesus,'" as appropriately interpreted by R.W. Dale.

This should remind us that access to the divine life does not in a moment, or in a flash, change a person's moral conduct and habits. We are to grow into the Lord. We are to be no more children *tossed to and fro*. The urgency, knowledge, and love of God's will will not be felt immediately in every area of one's life. Moral distinctions which were once nonexistent or at best very faint will not become vivid overnight.

We should not be surprised by this. When a person begins to grow in Christ, it does not mean the change will be immediate and complete: a violent temper being changed to gentleness, selfishness expanding into generosity, a suspicious nature becoming trusting, the vain person becoming modest, the proud person becoming humble, and the irresponsible person becoming responsible. These changes do not occur without the encouragement, support, strength, and knowledge available only in Christ Jesus. There is always a lag time, as evidenced in the parable of the father asking his two sons to work in the field.

The saints at Ephesus, when they acknowledged the authority of God and trusted in His love and power, did not immediately escape from the power and habits of their old life, and what is more, we did not either. Normally, Christian righteousness is achieved slowly. The fruit of the Spirit has to ripen according to God's plan and way. There is the growth, the bud, the flower, the fruit beginning to appear, the rain, the sun, the cold, the heat, the days and nights, then the maturing of the fruit and, at last, the availability, sharing, and enjoying of it. And one other thing: the planting of the seed so that more fruit will be borne.

There is a truth we are not to ignore or overlook: the only real growth and development of the fruit of the Spirit occurs where there is genuine loyalty to Christ, accompanied by a persistent effort to do the will of God as His will is known. As this occurs, a person will grow into Christ and become more like Him, while continuing to walk with Him and to learn from Him. The apostles loved Him and followed Him, but lest we forget, they learned and oh, how they learned from Him! They listened, they asked questions, they talked, they acted, and they grew in the Lord.

However, they had their lapses as they matured in their faith and witness, and so will we. Mark records that the disciples had forgotten Jesus feeding thousands with several loaves and a few fish shortly after it occurred. Also, he records that they could not cast out the dumb spirit from the man's son, whereas the father of the boy said, . . . *Lord, I believe; help thou mine unbelief* [Mark 9:24]. In addition, there is Peter's denial of our Lord Jesus the night He was betrayed. Then there is the occasion when Paul remonstrated Peter because he and others had . . . *walked not uprightly according to the truth of the gospel* [Gal. 2:14].

Who can forget the Apostle Paul saying, . . . *for what I would* (want to do)*, that do I not; but what I hate, that do I* [Rom. 7:15]. Maturing as Christ's disciples is not easy, as they may attest. There may be many obstacles to overcome, but the journey will be joyful since Christ Jesus will be our companion, guide, teacher, and strength.

Third, there is to be a constant linking of doctrine and practice, two sides to the same coin which is Jesus Christ. On the one side doctrine, on the other application, but at the center is the Master. You cannot get away from this truth.

As members of Christ's body we are to know how to conduct ourselves and understand the reasons for doing so. The Christian life is not a code imposed upon us. It is a relationship with the Lord Jesus Christ and the parameters He established.

It appears and matures out of doctrine. We are to understand the teachings and what we are to do or not to do. It is not because of a code or because of other people. It is because of Christ our Redeemer and friend. Remember, we are no more children! We are to learn, grow, and have understanding.

Our conduct should always be inevitable in view of what Christ taught. If it is not, something is amiss. This does not mean we will not stumble or fall in our actions. That is going to happen. However, it does mean that the desire to do as Christ would have us to do is paramount. Further, the more we learn, know, and understand, the more our conduct should be inevitable and in accord with Christ's example and teachings.

To amplify upon this, there is a difference between morality and Christian living. Morality is concerned about the rightness and goodness of the thing done in and of itself in terms of the social consequences. Is it good? Is it bad? What effect does it have? "There is a sense on which morality is a very insulting thing to a human being, it is only interested in my behavior," as Martyn Lloyd-Jones observed through the light of the Holy Spirit.

True Christianity is different from morality. Its primary focus is on God, our heavenly Father, and Jesus Christ, His Son, and the revelation of the Triune God to me through the power of the Holy Spirit. It is more concerned about me and my relationship to the Lord Jesus than in my conduct and behavior, not because it is good, bad, indifferent, or has an effect upon something else. It is interested in me because of my relationship to God and whether or not I am a member of Christ's body.

Fourth, the failure to live the Christian life, or life in Christ, ultimately results from the failure to understand the teachings of Scripture and the truth as it is found in Christ Jesus. If there is anger, malice, hatred, bitterness, or an unforgiving spirit, it is because we do not realize the Holy Spirit dwells within us, and we grieve Him when we succumb to these temptations. That is doctrine! We cannot go on being like that when we truly comprehend doctrine.

Hopefully, you comprehend that it is the failure to understand doctrine that results in the failure in practice or in living. We cannot ignore Christ's teachings and talk about being practical. Our conduct is determined to a large extent by Christ's teachings and our acceptance or rejection of them. That is why some people want to know the truth and some do not.

There is another point to consider: "It is unscriptural to be constantly making direct appeals to the "will" without inculcating doctrine," according to Martyn Lloyd-Jones.

Faith is the gift of God. When its embers are fanned it seeks understanding. The heart, mind, and will interact enabling a person to grasp certain truths, to understand them, and to increase in faith. Emotional appeals rarely lead to holiness. A personal growing relationship with Christ and acquiring an ever increasing understanding of His teachings and commands may lead to holiness. You do not achieve holiness by making a decision, but by increasing in understanding, effort, and prayer, and receiving the illuminating light of the Holy Spirit. What does this have to do with sanctification?

The teaching of sanctification is to be based upon doctrine and understanding, accompanied by an exhortation to apply the doctrine in a logical manner. Lest we forget or ignore Scripture, our sanctification is not the result of our own efforts, but requires God working within us through the Holy Spirit. The Apostle teaches sanctification from this seventeenth verse through the end of the letter. He does it by presenting the doctrine and urging the followers to work it out in detail and to apply it. This is contrary to the teaching that you can get it for nothing, that it is a gift, and that you have nothing to do.

We are to grasp Christ's teachings as He taught them and as the apostles taught them. Then we are to apply them. Our determination as members of Christ's body should not be the desire to be good, or better, or to eliminate certain sins, or to have happiness, or to be victorious.

Why should these things not be? Because it is a self-centered mindset and approach, which starts with me or with you, rather than with God the Father.

Paul says those self inflicted desires are not to be our concern, that is not where we are to start. What should we determine to be? To function fully and completely as a member of Christ's body. Our focus should not be that I am failing or having a problem, but that I am failing Him. I am not doing as He would have me to do. If I am not, then I am failing God and the body of Christ, which is His church. We need to move from being subjective and self-centered to being objective and Christ-centered.

We are to remember that He died for us, He wants us to be in the right relationship with God, and He wants us to be perfect and whole. People are concerned about themselves, their own problems, and their particular sins, and they pray about these things. They need to consider these things in terms of their relationship to Christ and being positive in so doing. Their objective should be to show the glory of Christ and His Church. *Let your light so shine before men, that they may see your good works, and glorify your Father which is in heaven* [Matt. 5:16]. You will note that our Lord did not stop with *Let your light so shine before men, that they may see your good works,* but He added *and glorify your Father which is in Heaven.* Their good works are to glorify the Father, not themselves.

We are to live in such a way that people may be puzzled by our conduct, not understand us, feel we are enigmas, or that we react differently. I say this on a positive, not negative, note. Because the people outside Christ will wonder why we do not act as they do. We must focus on our calling and our relationship to Christ as members of His body.

The Apostle in his letter to the Ephesians is leading us on the right path. We are to follow him in applying the teachings of that one great central truth, Jesus Christ is our Lord and Master, our Redeemer and Friend.

May we proceed from this day forth, walking with Jesus as exemplified in that beautiful, meaningful hymn, Lead On, O King Eternal by Ernest W. Shurtleff.

> *Lead on, O King Eternal, the day of march has come;*
> *Henceforth in fields of conquest thy tents shall be our home:*
> *Through days of preparation Thy grace has made us strong;*
> *And now, O King eternal, we lift our battle song.*

Lead on, O King eternal, till sin's fierce war shall cease,
And holiness shall whisper The sweet amen of peace;
For not with swords' loud clashing, Nor roll of stirring drums,
With deeds of love and mercy, The heavenly kingdom comes.

Lead on, O King eternal: We follow not with fears;
For gladness breaks like morning Where'er Thy face appears;
Thy cross is lifted o'er us; We journey in its light:
The crown awaits the conquest; Lead on, O God of might.

Amen!

2

The Vanity (Futility) of Their Mind

> *This I say therefore, and testify in the Lord, that ye henceforth walk not as other Gentiles walk, in the vanity* (futility) *of their mind, . . .* [Eph. 4:17].

The Scripture from Romans 1:18–25 is forceful, forthright, and enlightening. It relates to the material being considered throughout the remainder of Ephesians.

Paul deals with people according to where they have been, where they are, and where they will be. He vividly points out what they are not to be. Paul says, under the influence of the Holy Spirit, that we are to be something. His presentation in the first half of the fourth chapter deals with the unity and edification of His Church, which Christ has appointed. Then beginning with the seventeenth verse Paul tells them what they are not to do and what they are to do. He describes what fruit the teachings of Christ ought to bear and begins to explain the nature of the edification that should flow from doctrine.

Paul uses comparisons. This is seen in Ephesians and also in the first chapter of Romans. The first half of the latter is devoted to faith and to the righteousness that comes from that faith. Paul stresses that righteousness is bestowed upon us only through the Gospel. Then he demonstrates that without the Gospel a person is condemned. Further, that salvation is found in the Gospel and only in the Gospel. Paul notes that man by himself does not glorify God and that people in their natural condition are guilty of sacrilege and ingratitude.

The Apostle's objective is to instruct the followers as to where salvation is to be sought. It can be obtained only through the Gospel. Why does he emphasize this? Because the flesh will not willingly humble itself nor ascribe salvation to the grace of God alone. For us to fully understand this requires examining each word and the context in which it is presented.

Preachers and teachers for the most part wish to present the pleasant accounts and teachings of Scripture and to overstress the love of God, but that is not according to God's divine revelation presented in His Word. Teachers and pastors have no right to interpose their choices and priorities over divine revelation. The Apostle declares,

> *For the wrath of God is revealed from heaven against all ungodliness and unrighteousness of men, who hold* (suppress) *the truth in unrighteousness;*
> *Because that which may be known of God is manifest* (evident) *in* (among) *them; for God hath showed it unto them*
> [Rom. 1:18–19].

John Calvin expounds upon Paul's statement to the Romans saying, "[h]is object is to instruct us where salvation is to be sought. He has stated that we can obtain it only by the Gospel, but because the flesh will not willing humble itself to the point of ascribing the praise of salvation to the grace of God alone, Paul shows that the whole world is guilty of eternal death.

"Some interpretors distinguish between ungodliness and unrighteousness, maintaining that ungodliness refers to the profanation of the worship of God, and unrighteousness to a want of justice to men . . . One thing is designated by the two different expressions, viz. ingratitude to God, because we offend against God in two ways. . . . ungodliness implies a dishonouring of God, while . . . , unrighteousness, means that man by transferring to himself what belongs to God, has unjustly deprived God of His due honour."

Paul adds strength and enlightenment to this statement with his words to the Ephesian elders at Miletus, saying,

> *And now, behold, I know that ye all, among whom I have gone preaching the kingdom of God, shall see my face no more.*
> *Wherefore I take* (testify to) *you to record this day, that I am pure* (innocent) *from the blood of all men.*
> *For I have not shunned to declare unto you all the counsel of God*
> [Acts 20:25–27].

Paul refers to the words of Ezekiel when he addresses the elders from Ephesus,

> *Son of man, I have made thee a watchman unto the house of Israel: therefore hear the word at my mouth, and give them warning from me.*
>
> *When I say unto the wicked, Thou shalt surely die; and thou givest him not warning, nor speakest to warn the wicked from his wicked way, to save his life; the same wicked man shall die in his iniquity; but his blood will I require at thine hand.*
>
> *Yet if thou warn the wicked, and he turn not from his wickedness, nor from his wicked way, he shall die in his iniquity; but thou hast delivered thy soul.*
>
> *Again, When a righteous man doth turn from his righteousness, and commit iniquity, and I lay a stumbling block before him, he shall die: because thou hast not given him warning, he shall die in his sin, and his righteousness which he hath done shall not be remembered; but his blood will I require at thine hand*
>
> [Ezek. 3:17–20].

What God declares in Ezekiel about His prophet applies to pastors and teachers today. It explicitly says they are responsible if any perish due to their negligence or ignorance in presenting the Gospel. The account is to be paid by them, and those who go astray will be charged to them. That is an awesome responsibility for those who preach and teach!

God through His Word shows us how precious each person is to Him. Then because of their destruction He exacts a severe penalty from the lazy or indifferent pastors and teachers. Paul very explicitly says to the Ephesian elders, *For I have not shunned to declare unto you all the counsel of God* [Acts 20:27]. He did not choose the bits and pieces. He declared the whole counsel of God.

The righteousness of God is revealed from faith to faith, from the faith of one believer to the faith of another, but the wrath of God is revealed from heaven. The Holy Spirit has bestowed upon preachers and teachers the ability to tell people about God's grace, to proclaim the Gospel, and to communicate the faith, but wrath is from heaven; therefore, it is to be proclaimed by preachers and teachers. When considering God's Word, bear in mind that it is a privilege to announce faith and righteousness, but it is a duty to announce wrath and unrighteousness.

The truth as stated in these verses [Rom. 1:18–19] is the truth of God and means true knowledge of God. To hold down this truth is to suppress or obscure it. The phrase *who hold the truth in unrighteousness* actually means "to hold the truth of God unjustly and unworthily." Paul tells us what we are to know about God in order to glorify Him.

We are to focus attention on what Paul says,

> *This I say therefore, and testify in the Lord, that ye henceforth walk not as other Gentiles walk, in the vanity* (futility) *of their mind,*
> *Having the understanding darkened, being alienated from the life of God through* (because of) *the ignorance that is in them, because of the blindness* (hardening) *of their heart:*
> *Who being past feeling have given themselves over unto lasciviousness* (licentiousness), *to work all uncleanness with greediness* [Eph. 4:17–19].

When examining these words remember that as followers of Christ we are to be entirely new men and women. Regeneration has occurred and has brought about a profound change.

The true Christian is not someone who has decided to be a little more moral, or to join the church, or to participate in various functions. What makes a person a true Christian is having a new birth, being a new creature, putting on the new person. We are to remember that this has happened. As we continue our studies we will learn more about this and the impact it has upon our daily living.

The result of these events does not become evident immediately, but only as we progress, increase in knowledge and understanding, and mature in our daily walk with Christ. The transformation within the followers is gradual, the result of spiritual growth nourished by a personal relationship to Christ and the power of the Holy Spirit.

Paul begins this portion of Ephesians with these strong words, *This I say therefore, and testify in the Lord*. The word *testify* means "to bear witness" or "to solemnly enjoin" in the Lord. He makes it perfectly clear that it is not Paul's word, but that he is bearing witness to the Lord God Almighty. The phrase *in the Lord* means that he is testifying as one who is in the Lord, who is delivering an authoritative message, and who is speaking as one with access to the mind of God. The way Paul speaks here is different from when he says, *But I speak this by permission, and not of commandment* [1 Cor. 7:6].

When Paul speaks by his own reasoning or deduction he says so, but when he speaks with the full authority of an apostle he also says so. Paul says in the third chapter of Ephesians that this great and glorious doctrine was revealed to him. Also, the details regarding acceptable conduct were revealed to him. These teachings about daily living and conduct have the same divine, apostolic authority as the exposition of doctrine he previously presented.

Therefore, in these latter verses of Ephesians he is speaking as one clothed with the unique authority of the apostles. The followers in the Way are members

> . . . *of the household of God;*
> *And are built upon the foundation of the apostles and prophets,*
> *Jesus Christ himself being the chief corner stone* [Eph. 2:19–20].

To what is Paul testifying?

> *That ye henceforth walk not as other Gentiles walk, in the vanity* (futility) *of their mind,* . . . [Eph. 4:17].

First, the Apostle injects a negative. He tells them what they are not to do. It is not sufficient to tell people what they are to do. We must tell them what they are not to be and not to do. The first thing he says is that ye are not to walk as the other Gentiles do. This refers to their whole life, not only the tenor of it, but the details. The walk means both the inward and outward life.

Second, the word *henceforth* comes from the Greek word *mēketi* which is definite in its meaning. It means, "no more, not again, never again." Paul introduces the application of Christ's teachings with the admonition "no more, not again, never again." How can that be misinterpreted? Why does he say it this way? Because of the tremendous change that has taken place by the power of the Holy Spirit. He is saying what is past, is past. From now on things are different. The old things are passed away; behold, all things are become new.

The third negative is that they are to *walk not as other Gentiles walk.* He tells them they are now members of Christ's body; therefore, even though you are Gentiles you are not to walk as you once did. You are not to walk like that any more. Paul stresses that they are no longer what they once were. This is the point where people exclaim, *"Whereas I was blind, now I see"* [John 9:25]. This is where we are to rise up and praise God. Thank God we can have a new beginning, a new start, and a new life.

Fourth, he inserts a remarkable phrase when he says they are not to walk *in the vanity* (futility) *of their mind.* It is a tremendous yet terrible description of the unregenerate life of those who are not members of the household of God. Paul reminds the Ephesians that previously he told them,

> *Wherein in time past ye walked according to the course* (age) *of this world, according to the prince of the power of the air, the spirit that now worketh in the children of disobedience:*
> *Among whom also we all had our conversation* (conducted ourselves) *in times past in the lusts of our flesh, fulfilling the desires of the flesh and of the mind; and were by nature the children of wrath, even as others* [Eph. 2:2–3].

Paul tells them that their values, their ideals, and their conduct were in accord with the secular, nonbelieving people who did not believe in God and did not have a relationship with the Lord Jesus Christ. However, Paul does not leave it at that. He focuses their minds on what is true by saying,

> *But God, who is rich in mercy, . . .*
> *. . . hath quickened* (made alive) *us together with Christ, . . .*
> *And hath raised us up together, and made us sit together in heavenly places in Christ Jesus:*
> *That . . . he might show the exceeding riches of his grace in his kindness toward us through* (in) *Jesus Christ* [Eph. 2:4–7].

Paul was descriptive and forthright in his statements. He reminds them what their plight had been and to what they had been raised by God's grace through the Lord Jesus.

Naturally, the question may be asked: is the Apostle repeating himself in the fourth chapter? No, he is not. In the second chapter, he provides an objective lesson of life outside Christ and life in the pagan world. In the fourth chapter he gives a Christ-centered analysis of that life. Chapter two provides a general description, whereas chapter four dissects, analyzes, and exposes the source of it all. This is a profound analysis.

Paul beckons them to remove themselves from the vanity of unbelievers. He makes it clear that for those who have received the teachings of Christ and have been enlightened by the doctrine of salvation, it would be quite absurd to follow vanity and to be no different than nonbelievers. He reminds them that their lives should demonstrate having become disciples of Christ. And that is how they are to conduct themselves!

Why stress these negatives? This description and analysis is an accurate explanation of what is happening and being experienced in our modern world. The words of Paul nearly two thousand years ago are applicable to conditions today. These things do not change. They are eternal principles. Therefore, we are to understand the Apostle's teachings and recognize that evangelicals or reformers are criticized for: not being practical; not spending time discussing the scriptures; and not doing anything about the secular world or existing conditions. The simple truth is that you cannot do anything until you begin to understand Christ's teachings and commands. That is where you must start. To start anywhere else is a waste of time and will not produce lasting, beneficial results.

Paul attributes the gross ethical corruption of the Gentiles, the heathen, to their ignorance of God and the teachings of Christ. Their ignorance is the result of their unfaithfulness. This can be described in direct, understandable words that say, "Where there is irreverence for the divine law the vision of God becomes fainter; as the vision of God becomes fainter the restraints of the Divine righteousness are lessened, irreverence and disobedience become more and more flagrant and at last the vision of God is lost altogether," as appropriately and explicitly stated by R.W. Dale. How true!

Ruth Paxson, the missionary, provides, additional insight to Paul's message to the Ephesians (and us) in verses 17–19 of Chapter 4 stating that, "[i]t is a picture of: Spiritual death—being alienated from the life of God. Mental darkness—having the understanding darkened. Moral degeneracy—who being past feeding have given themselves over. Physical depravity—unto lasciviousness to work all uncleanness with greediness.

"The ignorance that was in them (and is seen today) through willful blindness of heart had produced an impotence which finally generated insensibility toward everything spiritual, ethical and moral. With deliberation and premeditation they had abandoned themselves to utter sensuality without any protest from conscience, reason or heart."

In this Epistle, Paul shows the origin of the evil life that he describes. "The Apostle asserts that you cannot have morality without godliness. There are people who are concerned about morality, but they are not concerned about godliness and righteousness. There have been people who have said over the past eighty to eighty-five years that morality is good. How you act and how you treat your neighbor is good, but we do not need godliness, we do not believe in the supernatural, we do not believe in miracles, and we do not believe that Jesus Christ is the Son of God. These people thought they could preserve morality without godliness. But you cannot!" as emphasized by Martyn Lloyd-Jones.

The Apostle stressed that the Gentiles should live in a certain way. However, he was much more concerned with the reasons why. People are concerned with the decline in morals. But, Martyn Lloyd-Jones asks: "why is this happening and what can be done about it?"

Broadly speaking, people have lost the knowledge of God and the knowledge of the steadfast, eternal laws of righteousness. We need to realize that we are surrounded by the invisible, divine, eternal world. It is not far off. We are to see beyond the immediate. We are to discover that what has been revealed to us by Christ is real and enduring. As members of the body of Christ, we are to see that man's true life is eternal and that true happiness is found in the eternal, divine kingdom.

What are we to do about evil? Denounce it? Say how horrible, how terrible it is? "The business of the Gospel is not simply to denounce. It is to deal with situations the only way it can by preaching the Gospel, the power of God unto salvation. That is the New Testament story. That is the only hope for society. You can let men do what they will, they can multiply their educational, moral, and social organizations, but they will not handle the situation of evil. The only way they can handle it is through the hearts of men and women hearing and knowing the Word of God," to quote and paraphrase Martyn Lloyd-Jones.

What does the Apostle mean by this? What does he mean by *the vanity* (futility) *of their mind*? Paul does not mean the mind only. The Greek word used in this verse is *nous* which means "the will as well as the mind." It includes the emotional capabilities as well as the reasoning, the understanding, and the conscience. Basically, it means the whole person. To put it another way, it means the entire outlook on life and the manner in which people live their lives.

But in this verse, the Apostle says that they walk *in the vanity* (futility) *of their mind*. The Greek word for *vanity* is *mantaiotes*, which means "uselessness." An alternative term is "emptiness." The Revised Standard Version interprets it as "the futility of their mind," which can be interpreted "utterly empty, absolutely futile." It means something that is aimless, pointless, and lacking in direction. That is what the Apostle is saying. It is not difficult to understand.

What Paul says about walking *in the vanity* (futility) *of their mind* applies to life as it was being lived both at that time and today. We find in the seventeenth chapter of Acts that the Athenians were interested in or talked about religion, truth, and God. They even had an altar with the inscription, *To the Unknown God*. They talked about it, but where did it lead them? The majority of their people were atheists, some were pantheists who believed that God was in everything, and others were polytheists who believed in the multiplicity of gods. They were people searching after God. Where did it lead them? To futility. They did not know Him. It did not lead to anything in a religious sense or in their personal lives.

Where did it lead them intellectually? The answer is the same. They had no satisfaction. They did not have any real understanding of people, life, and the purpose of life. They were interested in history, but not where they were going. They did not have the biblical concept of the one event to which the whole of creation is moving.

What was their view of death? To many of them, death was merely the end. There was not anything beyond the grave. Others believed in a series of reincarnations. Others thought that the state of man beyond the grave was elusive, vague, indefinite, and nebulous. Further, that there was a gloom and darkness about it. What was their outlook? Basically, unhappiness! Emptiness! Futility!

What was the outlook of the ancient world? A confession of futility; utter emptiness; going round in circles; no understanding of life; no knowledge of how to live; nothing to cheer them beyond the grave; and eat, drink, and be merry, for tomorrow we die. That was life in the ancient pagan world. That is life for many today.

When you think about it, is that not a description of life in this modern world without Christ? Where does it lead? In spite of our so-called progress during the past two thousand years, the description of the people in Ephesus at that time is true of the people in today's world. Life without Christ is always empty; it is always vain; it takes from you; and it takes out of you. It leaves you an empty husk with nothing to offer.

What then is the Apostle saying? You are no longer to be controlled and influenced by an outlook that does that to you. He says, no more, not again, never again! He says that concept of living is utterly empty, futile, aimless, and pointless. He says to the Ephesians (and to us), *I say therefore, and testify in the Lord, that ye henceforth walk not as other*

Gentiles walk, in the vanity (futility) *of their mind* [Eph. 4:17]. Thank God that He has opened our hearts and minds. The Apostle John says, *This is the victory that overcometh the world, even our faith* [1 John 5:4]. It is the Gospel; it is the faith that opens our eyes to the vanity of this world, its mind, its outlook, and its life.

How did this happen?

> *For unto you is born this day in the city of David a Saviour, which is Christ the Lord* [Luke 2:11].

Henceforth, no more, not again, never again was the world the same.
Amen!

3

Hardness of Their Hearts

> *This I say therefore, and testify in the Lord, that ye henceforth walk not as other Gentiles walk, in the vanity* (futility) *of their mind,*
> *Having the understanding darkened, being alienated from the life of God through* (because of) *the ignorance that is in them, because of the blindness* (hardening) *of their heart:*
> *Who being past feeling have given themselves over unto lasciviousness* (licentiousness), *to work all uncleanness with greediness* [Eph. 4:17–19].

One Christmas, I received a very meaningful letter from my oldest daughter and a devotional book entitled, "My Utmost For His Highest," by Oswald Chambers. The devotion for December 26 was most appropriate for our subject matter in Ephesians 4:17–19. The teachings we are focusing upon are:

- *walk not as other Gentiles walk, in the vanity* (futility) *of their mind,*

- *Having the understanding darkened, being alienated from the life of God through* (because of) *the ignorance that is in them,*

- *because of the blindness* (hardening) *of their heart,* and

- *Who . . . have given themselves over unto lasciviousness* (licentiousness), *to work all uncleanness with greediness* [Eph. 4:17–19].

Note the emphasis on blindness and darkness when they walk *in the vanity* (futility) *of their mind* and are *alienated from the life of God.*

Our scripture for December 26th was: *If we walk in the light, as he is in the light, we have fellowship one with another, and the blood of Jesus Christ his Son cleanseth us from all sin* [1 John 1:7]. *If we walk in the light*. This does not mean we walk in the light of our own intellects or consciences, but in the light of God, His Son, and His Word. It also means that the darkness, the haze, the hidden places are not to attract us. Walking in the light means everything that is of darkness should drive us closer to the center of the light.

Paul effectively uses contrasts in his letters. Where is there a greater contrast than between darkness and light? Paul incisively describes the darkness and its causes in these three verses, saying with emphasis and strength, *But ye have not so learned Christ* [Eph. 4:20].

Why do darkness and death go together? What causes the vanity or the empty-headedness of one's mind? How was man created? What is the chief end of man? These are questions to consider when examining this Scripture.

In these verses, the Apostle describes the condition of intelligent, sophisticated people who belittle Christian truths, who deride a sincere faith in Christ, and who boast in their own knowledge, learning, reasoning, and understanding. It is important to understand these people and how they achieved their status in darkness.

What happened to them? First, their understanding was darkened. Second, they were alienated from the life of God. Why were they estranged from God? The primary reason was the ignorance that was in their minds, or the blindness that was in their hearts, or both.

The complex structure of verses 17–19 makes it difficult to interpret whether the ignorance the Apostle speaks of is actual want of knowledge or whether it is a refusal to know and to learn. However, it was certainly because of a lack of knowledge, regardless of the real reason. Ignorance of the Bible and its message transcends the intellect or mind. It includes one's emotions, will, and conduct. It follows that if a person does not know the Lord, it may be said that he ignores Him.

In the Old Testament, Israel is accused of ignoring God, while in the New Testament the Gentiles are said to be guilty of this sin. In reality, it is ignorance of God's teachings, which amounts to suppressing the truth, repudiating God's revelation, and considering the knowledge of God as undesirable, unfit, or unnecessary.

When these matters are addressed, some people respond while others want to place the blame on external or circumstantial reasons. However, one must realize that he cannot place the blame outside of himself for something that originates within and dwells therein.

Scripture says these people have blindness in their hearts. The Greek word for *blindness* is *pōrōsis* which means "hardness." Therefore, this phrase should read "because of the hardness of their hearts." This word also means being "insensitive." The Ephesians had their understanding darkened because of ignorance, the hardness of their hearts, and being insensitive to the Gospel.

What does Paul mean by the word *understanding*? The Greek word is *dianoia*. It literally means "a thinking through or over," "a meditation," and "reflecting." It signifies the faculty of knowing and understanding, or moral reflection. In this instance, since there is an evil significance, it is a consciousness characterized by a perverted moral outlook.

In the context of this verse, Paul apparently means the intellect and understanding, as opposed to feelings, emotions, sensibilities, and the will. Previously, when Paul was talking about the vanity of their minds, he was referring to the whole person. In this verse, when talking about understanding, he means the intellect.

Paul, in 2 Corinthians, says,

> *And not as Moses, which put a veil over his face, that the children of Israel could not steadfastly look to* (look steadily at) *the end of that which is abolished* (was passing away):
> *But their minds were blinded* (made dull): *for until this day remaineth the same veil untaken away in the reading of the old testament; which veil is done away in Christ.*
> *But even unto this day, when Moses is read, the veil is upon their heart.*
> *Nevertheless, when it* (one) *shall turn to the Lord, the veil shall be taken away* [2 Cor. 3:13–16].

This shows how the blindness and hardness of the people was exhibited from the time of Moses. The people refused to look upon Moses until his face was veiled. Why? Because the brightness of Moses' countenance was a sign of God's glory. The veil was a sign of the future hardness of the Israelites. Their blindness kept them from realizing and enjoying the teachings of the Law. Their hardness did not last for the brief time that Moses wore the veil, but continued to the time of Christ and Paul. And it continues today.

Their understanding (mind) was blinded and hardened. This kept them from learning the real meaning and intent of the Law. Even today when the Law is preached or taught there are people who do not hear it and grasp it. They do not see the light that is in it. The Law only receives its light when Christ appears. The Jews and others, whether at Ephesus or other places, turned their eyes away from Christ. Therefore, it is not surprising that they refuse to look at the light, or use it to illuminate their way.

There is a significant truth contained in this section of Scripture, especially when Paul says, *Nevertheless, when it* (one) *shall turn to the Lord* (Christ), *the veil shall be taken away* [2 Cor. 3:16]. A veil had been placed on the Israelites when Moses read the Law to them and when they read the Law, themselves. When people turn to Christ the veil is taken away. Christ is the end of Law. However, when people exclude Christ from the Law, they are in reality turning from the Law. When they read the Law without seeing Christ, they wander in a maze trying to find their way to no avail.

Paul says that if the Jews or others seek Christ in the Law, then the truth of God will be revealed to them and it will apply to them. But if they wish to be wise without Christ they will wander in darkness, their hearts will be hardened, and they will never obtain the true meaning of the Law.

How does this apply to the whole of Scripture? When God's Word is not considered as referring to Christ, which is its one aim and objective, then the Word is distorted and perverted. The Apostle adds further emphasis to this truth when he says,

> *But if our gospel be hid* (veiled), *it is hid to them that are lost* (perishing):
> *In whom the god of this world hath blinded the minds of them which believe not, lest the light of the glorious gospel* (gospel of the glory) *of Christ, who is the image of God, should shine unto them.*
> *For we preach not ourselves, but Christ Jesus the Lord; . . .*
> *For God, who commanded the light to shine out of darkness, hath shined in our hearts, to give the light of the knowledge of the glory of God in the face of Jesus Christ* [2 Cor. 4:3–6].

The third verse says, *But if our gospel be hid* (veiled), *it is hid to them that are lost* (perishing). Calvin meaningfully interprets this saying, "that the blindness or hardness of the non-believers does not detract from the clarity of the gospel. The sun is no less bright because it is night, or because people do not receive its light."

When Christ is seen and included in the Law, then its light not only shines upon the hearers, but it illumines their hearts and minds. As a result, they have light on their pathway as they walk with the Lord.

Why do people live as they do in ignorance, darkness, and blindness, alienated from the life of God? Paul tells the Corinthians the reason is Satan and his impact upon non-believers, saying, . . . *the god of this world hath blinded the minds of them which believe not, lest the light of the glorious gospel* (gospel of the glory) *of Christ should shine unto them* [2 Cor. 4:4]. Paul tells the members of Christ's body in Ephesus that those who are not believers have the hardness of their hearts and minds controlled by Satan as well as their own self-centeredness. In addition, they are blind and cannot see . . . *the glorious gospel* (gospel of the glory) *of Christ*.

Scripture offers additional explanations in the Old and New Testaments. It is a failure in their minds, intellects, and understanding.

> *And this is the condemnation, that* (the) *light is come into the world, and men loved darkness rather than* (the) *light, because their deeds were evil* [John 3:19].

> *To open their eyes, and to turn them from darkness to light, and from the power of Satan unto God* [Acts 26:18].

It is the fundamental business of preaching and teaching that the hearers' eyes should be opened, not that they should be entertained. They are to go from darkness to light and knowledge. Jesus says, *I am the light of the world: he that followeth me shall not walk in darkness, but shall have the light of life* [John 8:12].

When delving into Scripture we find that the non-believer is one who is in darkness, who is blind, and whose understanding has become darkened. However, we are to walk in the light and to seek the light.

Many examples can be given of famous or well-known intellectual people who, despite their renown in other fields, remained in darkness with respect to living their lives as God intended, or did not understand the meaning of life. They did not understand the Bible, or its teachings. *For, behold, the darkness shall cover the earth, and gross darkness the people: but the Lord shall arise upon thee, and his glory shall be seen upon thee* [Isa. 60:2]. This is an accurate description of man outside Christ and not in a right relationship with Him.

Why is it that some people who appear to be, or are, intelligent say they do not believe in Christ and seem to delight in saying why they are not Christians? This has been true for two thousand years. You hear the same thing from those who are not as intelligent and those who are illiterate or uneducated. You hear it from all layers of society. Why? Paul describes the reasons:

> *That not many wise men after the flesh, not many mighty, not many noble, are called:*
> *But God hath chosen the foolish things of the world to confound* (put to shame) *the wise; and God hath chosen the weak things of the world to confound* (put to shame) *the things which are mighty;*
> *And base* (insignificant) *things of the world, and things which are despised, hath God chosen, yea, and things which are not, to bring to nought* (nothing) *things that are:*
> *That no flesh should glory in his presence* [1 Cor. 1:26–29].

Paul reveals an important truth in this statement: we are not to glory in what we may possess, since it all comes from God who has provided it through Christ. It is in this way that we receive wisdom, righteousness, sanctification, and redemption. Therefore, Paul's words are meaningful and true when he says, HE THAT GLORIETH, LET HIM GLORY IN THE LORD [1 Cor. 1:31]. Paul uses both the indicative and imperative to inform the Corinthians regarding this matter. Saying this is what happened, these are the facts, he is calling them to witness to something obvious, and he is confronting them with it right then and there. Using the imperative, he exhorts them to consider the very matter he is presenting to them.

Paul points out the manner of their calling. He advises them that if they despise the humility of the Cross, then they are in effect nullifying their call. God's call eliminates any possibility of a person boasting in human wisdom, power, or glory. Paul says that all those whose wisdom is on a purely human level have no taste for the teaching of the Gospel. This is due to their blindness. How does this detract from the Gospel?

When ignorant people disparage the Gospel, it usually occurs because they are echoing the comments of other people. Paul uses this to glorify the Spirit of God. He teaches that the Word is despised because men do not know it, they are ignorant about it. It is unknown because it is at one and the same time too profound and lofty to be grasped by the mind of the natural man. The natural man cannot have the slightest morsel. Paul implies that human pride causes men to ignore or to condemn that which they do not understand. The dullness of the human mind is not capable of spiritual understanding. Why?

Neither a person's pride nor the impotence of the natural mind can attain the things of the Spirit. Paul says that men not only do not wish to be wise, but they also do not have the power to do so by themselves. Faith does not depend upon our own decision; it is given by God.

The Spirit of God is the only true interpreter for revealing the Gospel message and its contents. Therefore, the minds of the natural men are in darkness until they are enlightened by the Holy Spirit. The light of reason, which is a necessity for all of us, is from the Spirit of God. God bestows the special gift of heavenly wisdom upon His sons, the heirs, the *joint heirs* with Christ.

This should make us realize "That there is much less ground for tolerating the ignorance of people who think the Gospel is offered universally to all men in such a way that it is free to everyone without distinction to lay hold of salvation by faith," as John Calvin appropriately warns Christ's disciples.

The spiritual person who has received a firm and sound knowledge of God's teachings is able to distinguish truth from falsehood and the teachings of God from the fabrications of men. The assurance of faith is not under the control of men. This prerogative is reserved to the Word of God and is declared to them so they will understand it. It cannot be obliterated or reduced to nothing by men.

The Apostle stresses to the Corinthians and the Ephesians (and to us) that we are enlightened by the Spirit to perceive the truth, equipped with a spirit of discernment to decide between truth and error, and able to decide what we should follow and what we should avoid.

Rightly, the question may be asked, why is the spiritual man endowed with so much light and capable of judging everything, especially when we are fallible and beset by ignorance in many areas, liable to do wrong, to fall, and to come to grief? How does Paul under the influence of the Holy Spirit handle this?

He does not make this ability apply to everyone and everything, especially when we are fallible, beset by ignorance, liable to do wrong, likely to fall and to come to grief. He says that human intelligence is useless for assessing the teachings of Christ and that the right to judge belongs to the Spirit of God alone and only to Him. We judge correctly and with assurance when we are born again, when God's grace is bestowed upon us, when we accept the teachings of Christ and God, and when the Holy Spirit reveals to us the truths of God in Christ.

Therefore, it is well to know and to remember before entering into battle or difficult situations to go to God first. We must not only pour forth everything that is within us, but we must also open our hearts and minds to be receptive to His will and wisdom. We must do both. We must strive to understand the will of God before venturing into unknown circumstances or tackling difficult assignments. We are to go forth only after seeking God's guidance and being prepared.

Throughout our life in Christ we come to difficult crossroads or dividing lines. At those times, we either procrastinate and veer toward a useless type of service to the Lord, or we become more useful and proceed to serve Him more effectively according to His will and for His glory.

The Apostle concludes the second chapter of 1 Corinthians with the phrase *But we have the mind of Christ* [1 Cor. 2:16]. It is not known whether Paul is speaking about believers in general or about ministers in particular. Either interpretation fits the context of the message. Calvin prefers that it means Paul himself and other faithful ministers. The Apostle says that God's servants are taught under the influence and direction of the Holy Spirit, and thereby this teaching is removed from human understanding. Therefore, those proclaiming God's Word are to speak it fearlessly as if it is conveyed with human understanding and proceeding from the mouth of the Lord. What is the result of so doing? God's Word spreads to all the believers and has an impact upon each and every one.

Paul says,

> *From whom the whole body fitly joined together and compacted* (knit together) *by that which every joint supplieth, according to the effectual* (effective) *working in the measure of every part* (each part doing its share), *maketh increase* (causes growth) *of the body unto the edifying of itself in love* [Eph. 4:16].

This exposition of Scripture enables us to understand why those outside the body of Christ ridicule the basic tenets of our faith—the incarnation, the miracles, the virgin birth, the substitutionary atonement, God punishing our sins in His Son, and the bodily Resurrection.

When the minds are darkened, when they don't have the light, they cannot comprehend the truth. Thank God that He calls people with all types of intellect, from all levels of society, and with every conceivable type of personality. When they come under the influence and power of the Holy Spirit, they begin to acquire understanding. Again, thank God that He calls all types.

When considering these truths, it is well to read again Paul's prayer at the close of the third chapter. This prayer is offered after Paul presents the Doctrine of Christ, but prior to the application of Christ's teachings. Probably, it has even more impact now than it did earlier. Paul prays,

> *. . . unto the Father of our Lord Jesus Christ,*
> *. . . That he would grant you . . . to be strengthened with might by his Spirit, . . .*
> *That Christ may dwell in your hearts by faith; that ye, being rooted and grounded in love,*
> *May be able to comprehend* (understand) *with all saints . . .*
> *And to know the love of Christ, which passeth knowledge, that ye might be filled with all the fullness of God* [Eph. 3:14, 16–19].

This is Paul's prayer, and we should continually offer the same praise and petitions to our heavenly Father. However, there are questions to consider at this point.

- Do we understand Paul's prayer?
- Do we believe this Gospel?
- Do we see why those who are not members of the body of Christ fail to understand the Gospel?
- Do we become impatient with those who do not believe?
- Do we become frustrated with those who cannot comprehend?
- Do we see why reasonable explanations fall on deafness?
- Do we begin to see something of the ignorance that is in them and the hardness that is in their hearts?

You can demonstrate the truth, you can argue and reason to perfection, but those who have their understanding darkened will see nothing. They cannot help themselves; they just cannot do it. We need to pray for them.

What are we trying to explain? There is only one thing that can remove the darkness and provide the light. That is the movement of the Holy Spirit. We can try as we will but to no avail. The Spirit must move.

Paul provides illumination, saying, *But God hath revealed them unto us by his Spirit: for the Spirit searcheth all things, yea, the deep things of God* [1 Cor. 2:10].

Paul shows that all men who are not believers and who have not been chosen are blind; the human mind is not able to rise up to a knowledge of God by itself. Paul shows that the faithful are delivered from darkness and blindness by the Lord honoring them with a special light from the Holy Spirit. Therefore, both the bright and dull minds are able to obtain understanding. If we do not understand these things, it is because our minds and intellects have been darkened.

If we understand, we have a grave responsibility and a demanding duty. We are to pray that the Holy Ghost will descend upon His church and that the preachers and teachers will present the truth in such a way that the hearers will hear it and understand it. We cannot do it; only the Holy Spirit can. We are to pray for the light of revival and for the Spirit to possess and to guide us. And we are to pray that the darkness will be removed and that we may walk with the Lord Jesus Christ in His light.

Amen!

4

Alienated from God

> *This I say therefore, and testify in the Lord, that ye henceforth walk not as other Gentiles walk, in the vanity* (futility) *of their mind,*
>
> *Having the understanding darkened, being alienated from the life of God through* (because of) *the ignorance that is in them, because of the blindness* (hardening) *of their heart:*
>
> *Who being past feeling have given themselves over unto lasciviousness* (licentiousness), *to work all uncleanness with greediness* [Eph. 4:17–19].

The Apostle in this remarkable analysis focuses on three things, which certainly are contrasts. First, we are to have a true understanding of the life alienated from God so that we may remove ourselves from it.

Second, "we are to understand and appreciate what God has done through His grace in delivering us from such a life. There is an old maxim that says those who have the deepest understanding of sin and what it does are those who have the greatest understanding and appreciation of God's love, grace, mercy, and kindness," to paraphrase Lloyd-Jones.

Third, we are to better understand those we know and with whom we come into contact who are not members of the body of Christ.

We live, work, and play among other people. If we are to be true evangelists and to witness effectively then we must understand those who are not in Christ. If we begin to comprehend the conditions around us and the power of God through the Holy Spirit, then we should spend more time in prayer, praying for true revival and the outpouring of the Holy Spirit upon ourselves and others. If we will do this, then the more we will pray for the ability to witness and to witness effectively.

The Apostle says, *being alienated from the life of God*. Consider what is meant by . . . *the life of God*. There were two words the Apostle could have used for *life* in this phrase. One is *bios*, which means "the manner, means, or period of life." However, he did not use this word.

The other word is *zōē* which means "life," "motion," "activity." This means life as a principle in the absolute sense. It is life as God has it, that is, which the Father has in Himself. It is also life which the Father gave to the Son *For as the Father hath life in himself; so hath he given to the Son to have life in himself* [John 5:26]. It is life with godliness, holiness, and righteousness; it is not merely a principle of power and mobility.

"It really means, in a sense, God's own life, the divine life . . . within us," as simply, yet meaningfully described by Martyn Lloyd-Jones. When men are alienated from the life of God, they are alienated from the life which is in God Himself and to the life which God gives to those believing in Him.

We have noted that the apostles support one another in presenting their teachings as revealed through Christ. Peter says,

> *Whereby are given unto us exceeding great and precious promises: that by these ye might be partakers of the divine nature, having escaped the corruption that is in the world through lust* [2 Pet. 1:4].

God's promises are to be given the highest possible value. They are free, they are offered as gifts, and we are to claim them. What is the value of these promises? They make us partakers of the divine nature. Is there anything more outstanding or ineffably sublime?

Think of it. God raises us up to a place of honor above all other creatures and those who know Him not. Our natural condition is worthless. Yet God makes Himself ours and bestows upon us all of His possessions. The magnitude of His grace is such that our minds can never fully grasp it. Paul wants us to realize that the purpose of the Gospel is to make us more Christlike. Peter amplifies upon this, saying, *According as his divine power hath given unto us all things that pertain unto life and godliness, through the knowledge of him that hath called us to* (by) *glory and virtue* [2 Pet. 1:3].

The apostles say that when we *put off* the lusts of the flesh we shall be partakers of divine immortality, God's blessed glory, and we shall be one with God according to the capacity bestowed upon us. Calvin stated it so eloquently, "The image of God in holiness and righteousness is reborn in us on the condition of our sharing in eternal life and glory."

Peter supports what Paul says in Ephesians. Therefore, if we grasp the truth as it is revealed to us and understand this one Epistle, we should know the whole doctrine of the Bible.

Paul says in these verses that life comes from God! Those who are not in Christ are strangers to that life and alienated from it. Our Lord stated it clearly and concisely and perfectly, saying,

> *And this is life eternal, that they might know thee the only true God, and Jesus Christ, whom thou hast sent* [John 17:3].

The people outside of Christ do not have this gift. They do not know the one true God. They do not know the Lord Jesus Christ. They are strangers, they are in darkness, and their hearts are hardened. And there is one more thing: they need our prayers that the Holy Spirit will move them.

What is meant by *the life of God*? One of two things: life in the sight of God or the life which God bestows upon His elect through the spirit of regeneration. There are three types of life in this world: (i) universal life, shared with animals and other creatures, which consists of motion and senses; (ii) human life or natural life, which is man's basic existence; and (iii) supernatural life, life in the Spirit, which the members of Christ's body receive.

Each life is received from God and may be called the life of God. In this instance, Paul is referring to the third type of life: the regeneration of the believers. Why? Because it is then that God lives in us, and in turn, we enjoy His life when He governs us by His Spirit.

Those who are not in Christ neither enjoy nor receive the blessings of that life. The life outside Christ produces things that are not of God. We must be renewed and infused with the grace of God before any true good can proceed from us. Remember, Jesus said,

> *Why callest thou me good? there is none good but one, that is, God: but if thou wilt* (want to) *enter into life, keep the commandments* [Matt. 19:17].

In this passage, Christ wants us to trust the authority of His teaching, hear God speaking, and exhibit an attitude of obedience. When our attention is called to something good, our thoughts should go to God and to Christ.

In studying Ephesians, we have observed that every word is important. The Authorized Version says, . . . *being alienated from the life of God*.

It should be interpreted, "having become alienated." It is not that they are alienated, but that they have become alienated. This is an important difference. Man has become estranged from God, whereas originally he was in communion and fellowship with our heavenly Father. Man has fallen from the life of God. This occurred in Adam. Jesus Christ came to restore us to the life of God. He can regenerate us.

The Greek word for regeneration is *palingenesia*. It means "new birth" or "again birth." Two powers produce this new life. First is "the word of truth." This is seen when James says, *Of his own will begat he us with the word of truth* [Jas. 1:18]. Peter supports this saying, *Being born again, not of corruptible* (perishable) *seed, but of incorruptible* (imperishable), *by the word of God, which liveth and abideth forever* [1 Pet. 1:23]. Second is "by the Holy Spirit." This is seen early in John's Gospel when Jesus encountered Nicodemus, who asked the Lord,

> *How can a man be born when he is old?...*
> *Jesus answered, Verily, verily I say unto thee, Except a man be born of water and of the Spirit, he cannot enter unto the kingdom of God.*
> *That which is born of the flesh is flesh; and that which is born of the Spirit is spirit* [John 3:4–6].

There are two questions at this point. What happens to the person alienated from the life of God? Why is this person *being* (having become) *alienated from the life of God*?

The person *being alienated from the life of God* seeks to worship something. Therefore, he makes his own gods or idols. He may worship self, money, family position, country, or whatever. There is something within that person that drives him or her to worship something. But there is something unique about the gods or idols man creates: they never satisfy!

The words of Jeremiah are so true: *For my people have committed two evils; they have forsaken me the fountain of living waters, and hewed them out cisterns, broken cisterns, that can hold no water* [Jer. 2:13].

Unfortunately, man *being alienated from the life of God* does not see, know, or understand his need for God, for the knowledge of God, and for life in God.

Our prayer should be as expressed by the psalmist,

> *AS the hart panteth after* (deer longs for) *the water brooks, so panteth my soul after thee, O God.*
> *My soul thirsteth for God, for the living God...* [Ps. 42:1–2].

St. Augustine stated it beautifully, "Thou hast made us for thyself, and our hearts are restless until they find their rest in thee."

These thoughts should lead us to ask and answer some simple questions. Do I know God? Am I sharing my life with Him? Have I found the fount of living water? Why is a person alienated from God? As discussed previously, it is through the ignorance that is in them, *because of the blindness* (hardening) *of their hearts*. Of what are they ignorant and blind?

They do not know God, nor the truth about Him. Further, they do not know the glory of God, nor His majesty. They do not know the holiness of God. Moses stated it so accurately,

> *Who is like unto thee, O Lord, among the gods* (mighty ones)*?*
> *Who is like thee, glorious in holiness, fearful in praises, doing wonders* [Exod. 15:11]*?*

They do not think of His righteousness and justice. *Thy righteousness is like the great mountains* (of God)*; thy judgments are a great deep* (ocean) [Ps. 36:6]. They do not acknowledge God's power to create and to sustain. *IN the beginning God created the heaven and the earth* [Gen. 1:1]. They do not think of God's love, mercy, and the exceeding riches of His grace, nor of the unsearchable riches of Christ.

Think of it! Men are ignorant of God's character, His love, and His attributes. In addition, they are ignorant of His purposes and His dispensations. They are ignorant of His plan and purpose for the world, the Old and New Testaments, and the will of God. That it is God's world that He controls in His own way; that it is His redemption, restoration, and regeneration; that if they die outside of Christ, they will remain there for eternity; that they are to know the truths of God and the teachings of Christ. I do not intend to be negative but to state succinctly why a person is *being alienated from the life of God*. This is an important truth to understand.

They do not know, and what is more significant, they do not want to know. Hosea stated it clearly and forcefully,

> *My people are destroyed for lack of knowledge: because thou hast rejected knowledge, I will also reject thee, that thou shalt be no priest to me: seeing thou hast forgotten the law of thy God, I will also forget thy children* [Hos. 4:6].

They are . . . *being* (having become) *alienated from the life of God* because of their ignorance, blindness, and hardness, and they do not know Him.

What are we to do? We are to tell people about the love of God in Christ Jesus and by our own lives convey how God's grace has changed us. We are not to stress happiness or peace or things appealing to an individual's desire. However, we are to stress knowing God and knowing Christ. Then the other things will follow. God comes first, then self. Paul adds emphasis to this when he says to the Ephesians, *Who being past feeling have given themselves over unto lasciviousness* (licentiousness), *to work all uncleanness with greediness* [Eph. 4:19].

What does the Apostle mean when he says *being past feeling*? He meant they were no longer sensitive to the obligations of truth, honesty, kindness, and purity. They were callous, guilty of falsehood, injustice, cruelty, or sensual sin. They could commit the grossest crimes and vices, yet they did not feel any shame, nor were they conscious of any wrongdoing. Does that sound familiar?

They were without any feeling with respect to the nobleness and beauty of virtue. There was nothing to restrain them from the vices that destroy. Their state or condition was such that they were beyond shame, regret, or remorse. The Lord spoke to Jeremiah regarding the obstinacy of the people, saying,

> *Were they ashamed when they had committed abomination? nay, they were not at all ashamed, neither could they* (did they know how to) *blush: therefore they shall fall among them that fall: at the time that I visit* (punish) *them they shall be cast down, saith the Lord.*
>
> *Thus saith the Lord, Stand ye in the ways, and see, and ask for the old paths, where is the good way, . . . But they said, We will not walk therein.*
>
> *Also I set watchmen over you, saying, Hearken to the sound of the trumpet. But they said, We will not hearken.*
>
> *Hear, O earth: behold, I will bring evil* (calamity) *upon this people . . . because they have not hearkened unto my words, nor to my law, but rejected it.*
>
> *To what purpose cometh there to me incense* (frankincense) *from Sheba? . . . your burnt offerings are not acceptable, nor your sacrifices sweet unto me.*
>
> *Therefore thus saith the Lord, Behold, I will lay stumbling blocks before this people, and the fathers and the sons together shall fall*

> *upon them; the neighbor and his friend shall perish* [Selections from Jer. 6:15–21].

Jeremiah says their condition had become such that they could not even blush. They had no feelings. They had no knowledge. They were ignorant. They had become beset with greed and had turned to idolatry. Sound familiar?

Therefore, the Lord said He would erect stumbling blocks, since they would not hearken to His words, and would bring about their destruction. When writing to Timothy, Paul echoes the words of the Lord in Jeremiah, saying,

> *NOW the Spirit speaketh expressly, that in the latter times some shall depart from the faith, giving heed to seducing* (deceiving) *spirits, and doctrines of devils:*
> *Speaking lies in hypocrisy; having their conscience seared with a hot iron* [1 Tim. 4:1–2].

What does this mean? The Greek word used for *seared* means "burned with a hot iron." Their consciences were cauterized, the tissue was destroyed. They no longer had feeling, they no longer had sensitivity, they could not respond positively, they had departed from the faith, they had given heed to seducing spirits to the doctrines of devils, and they did not want to know God.

There are two points Paul conveys when he says, *Speaking lies in hypocrisy; having their conscience seared with a hot iron*. Their bad consciences are burned by their evil deeds. When this occurs they resort to hypocrisy to hide what they have done, and they try to deceive God. They try to please God with their false, external observances.

The word *hypocrisy* in this verse must be taken in its context and considered in relation to doctrine. It means "that kind of doctrine which substitutes bodily gestures for God's spiritual worship and thus adulterates its genuine purity," according to John Calvin. This hypocrisy includes all the various ways that man has devised or invented to appease God, to obtain His favor, or to fool Him. True worshippers worship Him in spirit and in truth. However, these people were *past feeling*.

What other factors contribute to this condition of *being past feeling*? They want to say there is no such thing as a godly conscience; they argue against or reject the biblical view of sin and life; they say they must be able to express themselves, to do their own thing, to be free; they erect a façade; and they reach a point where they start to lose feeling, then they become numb, and finally they are past feeling. Paul says they gave *themselves over unto lasciviousness,* which means excess, licentiousness, absence of restraint, indecency, and wantonness.

The Apostle says *gave themselves.* They did it deliberately; they did not have any restraints on themselves. They were not betrayed, they were not forced, they were not overcome, nor did they resist until they became weary and finally yielded. Does this sound familiar? They abandoned all restraint, all attempts of self-control and discipline. They gave themselves up to this type of life, but guess what? That was not the end of it! They worked at it! They worked at *all uncleanness* and they did it *with greediness.*

In this verse, *uncleanness* means "lewdness," "unchastity," and "impurity." In other words, all the foulness of life. How direct Paul was! How we need it today! And to this he added the words, *with greediness,* meaning "a sense of selfishness" and "an impurity" that includes but is not restricted to sexual disorders and perverse actions.

This greediness includes covetousness and extortion. A simple definition is "Self is everything, nothing matters but self," according to the eminent twentieth century pastor/preacher Martyn Lloyd-Jones. Further, "I must have what I want, when I want it, and the more the better." Greediness is always out for self. If anything gets in the way, then move it out of the way, and do it quickly. When there is ignorance and blindness, they abandon themselves. As Paul says, *Have given themselves over unto lasciviousness* (licentiousness)*, to work all uncleanness with greediness.*

What does this say about the godliness of those who are in Christ, or profess to be? There is a strong belief prevalent among many that we have inherited virtues from our parents, that we have been disciplined and influenced for the good by our environment, and that moral and ethical conduct is only natural.

Therefore, it is assumed when a person joins the church that there is no reason for any great change in his or her habits. There may be some defects in a person's temper or some other area, but if he or she has lived among good, moral people, then their moral character is what it should be. Consequently, he or she thinks little about Christlike discipline and does not even consider that he or she needs to develop new foundations, new standards, different ideals, and different comparisons.

This is true even though he or she may attend church frequently, read the Bible and pray often, and perform tasks within the congregation. When this happens the result is that the ethical life among church members is no higher than in the outside world.

If the moral and ethical life of the members of the body of Christ is not governed by the teachings of Jesus and the conduct of His life, then the power of the church is impaired. There should be a distinct difference between the godliness of those in Christ and the moral or ethical standards of those who are not.

Paul vividly describes the life of those *alienated from the life of God*. He does not say that everyone outside Christ is guilty of all these evils. But he describes that type of life as a whole and says you are not to participate in it in the least way. You are not even to put your toe in the water, let alone swim in it.

- Does Paul's description help us to see the world a little better?
- Does it help us understand people both in and out of the congregation?
- Does it provide us with more knowledge and a better understanding of what God requires?
- Does it enable us to see life alienated from the life of God?
- Does it provide light instead of darkness?
- Do we begin to see the contrast and the importance of it?

If the answer is a resounding "Yes" to these questions, then we are ready to proceed to consider the next truth, *But ye have not so learned Christ* [Eph. 4:20].

Amen!

5

Contrasts

In Christ—Outside Christ

> *But ye have not so learned Christ;*
> *If so be that ye have heard him,*
> *and have been taught by him, as the truth is in Jesus*
> [Eph. 4:20–21].

Our Scripture is *But ye have not so learned Christ.* How do we learn Christ?

One thing is certain, we do not learn Christ by:

- ignoring Him,
- deliberately turning our backs on Him,
- refusing to learn about Him,
- not studying His teachings,
- not praying,
- accepting the standards established by man and abiding by those measurements and criteria, or
- using our own mindset as the barometer.

No, we do not learn Christ that way! The question is, how do we learn Him?

The first thing to do is to look at Scripture. By this I do not mean read it hurriedly or gloss over the words, but to study, examine, and digest it. What did the early followers do? Luke reveals in Acts that

> *They continued steadfastly in the apostles' doctrine and fellowship, and in breaking of bread, and in prayers* [Acts 2:42].

Also, the apostles testified to them and exhorted them, and many were baptized.

Please note what he said in these verses: he testified to them; he exhorted them; they received his words; they were baptized; and they continued steadfastly in the apostles' teaching, fellowship, the breaking of bread, and prayers. The forty-second verse says, *And they continued steadfastly.* The Greek word for *continued* means "to persevere toward a thing." They persevered. They did not leave the fellowship.

Luke reveals that those who accepted Christ readily and cheerfully embraced His words. Faith begins with a ready and willing desire to obey God's commands. However, we must recognize that some people exhibit a willingness at the beginning, but they do not persevere. Luke commends the three thousand because they willingly embraced the Word, they were joined to the disciples, and they persevered in doctrine.

He commends the followers for their constancy, because they persevered in those things, thereby strengthening their faith: they heard and studied the teachings of the apostles; they spent time in prayer; they maintained fellowship as members of Christ's body; and they continued in the breaking of bread. How else did they learn Christ?

Consider what Paul said to *the elders of the church* at Ephesus when he met with them in Miletus. He reminded them, saying,

> *How I kept back nothing that was profitable unto you, but have showed you, and have taught you publicly, and from house to house,*
> *Testifying both to the Jews, and also to the Greeks, repentance toward God, and faith toward our Lord Jesus Christ* [Acts 20:20–21].

The followers at Ephesus benefited immeasurably from Paul's presence and his ministry to them. He was in Ephesus for three years. He tells them in Miletus that he *kept nothing back, . . . taught you publicly, and from house to house, Testifying . . . repentance toward God, and faith toward our Lord Jesus Christ.*

That faithful member of Christ's body, Ruth Paxson, states when Paul met with the elders from the church at Ephesus in Miletus that "We may be very sure that Paul's teaching went beyond the elementary truths of salvation and included the deep, essential truth of sanctification through oneness of life with Christ. The mature, spiritual life of the church at Ephesus was, no doubt, the product of such painstaking, systematic indoctrination of full salvation in Christ. Oh, that every pastor, Bible teacher and missionary did the same today! The need for such indoctrination in the twentieth century (and today) is as great as it was in the first century church."

Paul exhibited three important characteristics in teaching the Ephesians: he gave them sound and thorough instruction, omitting nothing pertinent to their salvation; he did not limit his instruction to general preaching, but took the steps necessary to inform individuals carefully and deliberately; and he summarized his whole teaching by urging them to repent and to have faith in the Lord Jesus Christ.

Consider these three points in more detail. First is *sound and thorough instruction*. What should be done in this area? A faithful pastor and teacher should labor for the upbuilding of the church, which Paul did. He urged Timothy to reflect on the things beneficial to the followers, saying,

> *If thou put the brethren in remembrance of these things, thou shalt be a good minister of Jesus Christ, nourished up in the words of faith and of good doctrine, whereunto thou hast attained* (carefully followed) [1 Tim 4:6].

Scripture must be the norm for all teaching. It is the only basis for proper teaching and instruction. This means the whole of Scripture, not just selected portions. We need to learn the negatives, as well as the positives, the plusses and the minuses, and what we are to do as well as what we are not to do. Preachers and teachers are not to feed their members continually with milk and honey. They are to serve meat, some tough meat, as well as some tart food, and even some vinegar. The teacher is to serve a balanced diet, and the students are to ingest it. Everything cannot be taught at once.

However, progress is to be made, and we are to increase in knowledge and understanding day by day and year by year. Paul denies that he ever refrained from telling people those things that were for their benefit. Therefore, we should appreciate the fact that a pure, candid, and straightforward presentation of sound doctrine is required from Christ's servants. As Paul said, *If thou put the brethren in remembrance of these things, thou shalt be a good minister of Jesus Christ* [1 Tim. 4:6].

The second is *from house to house*. Paul taught the members of Christ's body in Ephesus not only in public assembly or worship, but also in their homes. The teaching in the home was according to each man's need. Christ taught that His disciples and ministers should teach from a public platform, as has happened throughout the centuries, but also they should care for the individual sheep.

It is safe to say that Paul's teaching extended beyond the elementary truths of salvation. It included the essential, basic truths of sanctification through unity, or oneness, with the life of Christ as members of His body. This is just as true today as it was in Paul's day in Ephesus. Oh, that every teacher and pastor did the same today. There is a great need for indoctrination, and the will to be indoctrinated in this day and in these times.

But ye have not so learned Christ; If so be that ye have heard him, and have been taught by him, as the truth is in Jesus. Paul says this regarding the process of teaching, hearing, and learning. Earlier in Ephesians an emphasis was placed upon *the Word* being proclaimed. Now we are involved not only with the teacher speaking, but with the listeners hearing and learning. While the Greek text does not explicitly mention a school or students, there is an indication in the vocabulary that a school or formal method of teaching was meant. Calvin has commented on this, saying, "teaching received in Christ's school."

> It is written in the prophets, AND THEY SHALL BE ALL TAUGHT OF GOD. Every man therefore that hath heard, and hath learned of the Father, cometh unto me [John 6:45].

The third is *Testifying both to the Jews, and also to the Greeks* [Acts 20:21]. Paul urged the Ephesians to faith and repentance. From Paul's words we learn that we must exert continuous effort to edifying God's word and making progress in His school. Paul uses the word *testifying* to provide greater emphasis and to remove any excuse for ignorance. In this instance, Paul is alluding to the law courts where testifying is introduced in order to eliminate all or any doubt. *Testifying both to the Jews, and also to the Greeks, repentance toward God, and faith toward our Lord Jesus Christ* [Acts 20:21]. Paul says that the people must be taught, they are to embrace salvation in the Lord Jesus Christ, and they are to yield themselves to God for newness of life.

He wanted the Ephesians to repent and to have faith. Repentance and faith are inseparably entwined. When God illuminates someone with the spirit of faith, He also regenerates the person with new life. Repentance is turning around. It is turning to God and being obedient to Him. Faith is receiving the grace of God that is presented in Christ Jesus.

Why does he stress repentance and faith? First, to serve the Lord purely, and to devote ourselves to holiness and righteousness. Second, to seek salvation only in Christ and in Him alone.

The teaching of repentance contains within it the rule of godly living. Because we are *alienated from the life of God* by nature and have a feeling of hostility toward Him, there must be a way of reconciliation. That is where faith ties in with repentance. Therefore, it is important to teach and to learn regarding:

- the promised forgiveness of our sins and our rebellion to the will of God;
- God's gracious adoption of those who were previously opposed to Him;
- the spirit of regeneration that comes only from the glorious Father;
- how godliness, righteousness, and uprightness must be drawn from the Father; and
- the process of implementation requires dependence upon God, plus His power, might, and strength.

Faith makes us friendly to God. By faith God washes away our sins and restores us to His image.

When reading Acts 20:21, you will note that Paul places repentance first, saying, *repentance toward God,* then *faith toward our Lord Jesus Christ.* Why did he do so? Not because one is superior or more important than the other, but because the act of repentance is the preparation for faith. We begin our repentance by being dissatisfied with ourselves and beginning to see the need for God. Throughout Scripture the objective of our faith is Christ. He is the goal toward which we are to progress. Therefore, our faith must be continuously fixed upon the Lord Jesus Christ.

Consequently, we are to learn Christ. The central theme of Paul's teaching is Christ. He has endeavored to bring Him to them in all His glory, righteousness, and full life. Paul taught the Ephesians, and they learned that they were to be Christlike, and to have Christ living in them.

Previously, Paul discussed being alienated from God and outside of Christ. Then, as was his custom, he presented a startling contrast, saying, *But ye have not so learned Christ* [Acts 4:20]. To show the contrast, he uses the little word *but*. Following this little word, he expresses three specific ideas.

The first idea is *ye have not so learned Christ,* or a translation is "you have not so learned the messiah." This phrase "to learn a person" is not found anywhere else in the Bible. It means more than just learning of His existence, or that He had made known certain teachings. There are other texts in the Bible that state Jesus Christ is *preached, known, received,* or *believed*. However, this verse states that Christ Himself is the subject of learning; that we are to learn Him, not just about Him.

"The central theme of Paul's teaching is perfectly clear. It had been such as to bring them Christ Himself in all the loveliness of His righteous, holy life. They had learned that to be a Christian is to have Christ in them living out His life again on earth in His mystical Body as He had lived it as Jesus in His earthly body," as described by Ruth Paxson.

The next idea to ponder is, *ye have heard him*. The Ephesians did not hear Christ during His earthly ministry, nor did they see Him. Yet Paul says, *ye have heard him*.

> *Since ye seek a proof of Christ speaking in me, which to you-ward is not weak, but is mighty in you* [2 Cor. 13:3].

This verse underscores Christ speaking through Paul when he says, *Christ speaking in me*. Calvin interprets this phrase as, "Christ, by exercising His power toward you in my teaching, has proved that He speaks through my mouth so that there is no excuse for your ignorance."

Paul does not boast in words, but proves that Christ speaks through him. He convinces the Corinthians that they should listen to him and to his claims. When it becomes clear that it is God's Word being proclaimed, then what Paul says holds true: if people do not believe, then they are disbelieving God. This is true of preachers and teachers, as well as the hearers of the Word.

The Apostle Paul demonstrates that when a minister or teacher effectively presents "the truth" as it is found in Jesus Christ and effectively discharges his duties, then there is no room for the hearers to evade or ignore the Word being proclaimed.

The third phrase in this grouping is *and have been taught by him, as the truth is in Jesus* [Eph. 4:21]. The words *in Christ* are equivalent to the words, "by Christ," since Jesus is definitely understood to be the teacher. *But ye have not so learned Christ* clearly indicates that He is the ultimate objective of the teaching. This is emphasized and duplicated by the words *the truth is in Jesus*. Also, Christ is the foundation upon which the teaching and learning are to take place. This is important, the teaching and learning are to take place only upon the one true foundation, that being Jesus Christ Himself.

The truth, the highest truth, we are to know as followers of Christ is in Jesus. The truth is in Him. The truth cannot be known if it is separated from Him. "All real and effective teaching must be in harmony with truth as truth is in Him," explained R. W. Dale. This truth is what the Apostle taught the Ephesians and what he teaches us.

When we stop, look, and consider the statement *But ye have not so learned Christ*, several thoughts come to mind. First and foremost, we should have a feeling of relief and thanksgiving. We should thank God that we are not *alienated from the life of God*. We should profess our profound gratitude to God that He has called us and blessed us.

Yes, He has called us in the midst of the world in which we live. He has called us to be members of the body of Christ, and He has provided for us. In the midst of the darkness around us there is a glimmer of light. In the midst of the multitude there is a remnant. Thank God there is light and there is a remnant.

Second, there is emphasis on learning Christ and learning the Gospel, *the truth is in Jesus*. This Gospel speaks to those called living and working in secular environments.

The Gospel comes as a contrast. It is not an extension of human philosophy; it is not an addition to something that men have been able to develop for themselves. The Gospel comes from God; it's His plan, His Good News. It comes in the midst of darkness, hopelessness, and despair, and it comes purely through the mercy and grace of God.

What about conditions early in the twenty-first century? We have a history of five thousand years and have seen everything that man has been able to propose, and what do we find?

- Is politics able to deal with the moral situation or international affairs?
- Is education able to do it?
- Are social agencies able to do it?
- Is money able to do it?
- Are handouts able to do it?
- Is freedom from work able to do it?
- Is anything man does able to reconcile man to man?
- Is anything able to eliminate the darkness or to overcome a darkened heart?

The answer to all these questions is No, a *resounding* No!

There is only one thing! Paul said it, *I am not ashamed of the gospel of Christ: for it is the power of God unto salvation to everyone that believeth* [Rom. 1:16]. Since it is the power of God it provides hope for everyone. The power of God is able to overcome the darkness, the hardness, and *being* (having become) *alienated from the life of God*. Why? Because it is the power of God, and there is no other power like it. It can make men new; it can refashion them.

The Apostle uses the words *But ye* at the beginning of the twentieth verse of the fourth chapter to show the contrast between those who are outside Christ and those who are in Christ. The business of Christianity is not to improve the world. It is to save people from it, and to form a new realm, a new kingdom, and a new humanity. They were to learn Christ so that the powers of the world could not prevail against them.

We must realize this: Scripture does not teach Christianizing the world. People are to be taken out of the world, even though they move and have their being in it.

> *But ye are a chosen generation, a royal priesthood, a holy nation, a peculiar* (his own special) *people; that ye should show forth* (proclaim) *the praises of him who hath called you out of darkness into his marvelous light:*

> *Which in time past were not a people, but are now the people of God: which had not obtained mercy, but now have obtained mercy.*
>
> *Dearly beloved, I beseech you as strangers and pilgrims, abstain from fleshly lusts, which war against the soul;*
>
> *Having your conversation* (conduct) *honest* (honorable) *among the Gentiles: that, whereas they speak against you as evildoers, they may by your good works, which they shall behold, glorify God in the day of visitation* [1 Pet. 2:9–12].

We are in this world, but we do not belong to it. We do not belong to its mind, its outlook, its organizations. We are strangers and pilgrims. We are merely here on a passport. Our Lord said in His high priestly prayer, *they are not of the world, even as I am not of the world* [John 17:14]. This does not mean that we should not participate in civic affairs or other secular events and organizations, but that the essence of the person in Christ is different, and so is his outlook.

The person in Christ knows that this is still God's world, and that God is going to redeem it. Of course, the person in Christ believes that sin and evil must be controlled. He realizes that politics and culture are designed to keep sin and evil within bounds and to keep them from running riot. He does not put his faith in earthly things, or in a social gospel.

Why? Because these things have always failed, and they always will because they are based upon the fallacy of not realizing that a man's heart is darkened and hardened. The only way it can be changed is by the power of God.

Paul says, *But ye have not so learned Christ.* When you learn Christ you cannot go on living as you did before. You cannot have your understanding darkened; there cannot be blindness in your heart. It is impossible. When you believe in Christ you cannot go on believing as you did without Him.

When the Apostle says, *ye have not so learned Christ* after describing life alienated from God, he is stating that it is impossible, it is unthinkable, it is ludicrous to believe a person can hold onto that way of life after becoming a member of Christ's body. The life in Christ is in contrast to everything represented by the world, by life, or existence. The life of the person in Christ is not vague and indefinite, nor difficult to define or recognize.

According to Paul's teachings and the rest of the New Testament, the life of the person in Christ should be recognizable. Christ Himself provided us with a few memorable descriptions appropriately saying, *. . . ye are the salt of the earth* [Matt. 5:13]. He is telling us that we are to "meet the needs of the world" and in so doing to add [appropriate] flavoring, act as a preservative, melt coldness, and heal wounds," according to the King James Study Bible. Jesus also says, *Ye are the light of the world* [Matt. 5:14]. He is giving us a commission. Since we are His, we are to provide light wherever we may be and with whomever we may associate. But, it is to be a special light in accord with His commands and teachings.

Paul asks the Corinthians, *. . . what fellowship* (in common) *hath righteousness with unrighteousness?* The answer is obvious—nothing! Paul provides encouragement for us to strive for righteousness, saying boldly, *. . . ye are the temple of the living God; as God hath said, I WILL DWELL IN THEM, AND WALK IN THEM; AND I WILL BE THEIR GOD AND THEY SHALL BE MY PEOPLE* [2 Cor. 6:16].

Paul says to the Ephesians that it is unthinkable for the followers of Christ to live as the nonbelievers do. Your whole life and behavior, your demeanor and deportment should bear witness to being a member of the body of Christ. People should know that we are different and that we have *so learned Christ*.

There is to be a line of demarcation between the church and the world. It is not to be obscured. This does not mean that we are not to mix with the publicans and sinners. However, we are not to be mistaken for one of them.

We are to show that we have learned Christ. He is the message, the teacher, the lesson, and the school. He is the headmaster, the teaching matter, the method, the curriculum, and the academy. He is the all in all. When we learn this, then we will learn Christ.

Then we will grow in Christ, we will be in Christ, we will walk in Christ, and we will realize the truth in Christ. We are to hear and accept the fact that *the truth is in Jesus*, then we are to live, act, and speak according to the standard as it is found in the Lord Jesus Christ. There can be no compromises, no divided interests. As Scripture says, *Ye were, Ye are, Become ye.* The power comes from God. It is through this power that we learn Christ and are changed.

Amen!

6

Knowing the Truth

Hearing and Learning Christ

> *But ye have not so learned Christ;*
> *If so be that ye have heard him, and have been taught by him, as the truth is in Jesus* [Eph. 4:20–21].

When examining all the complexities and intricacies that might have made a difference in our lives, then other thoughts permeate our minds. But when you come down to the bottom line there are some simple truths that can be stated. God sent Christ into the world, He ministered to the world, He went to the Cross obediently and willingly, and He instructed and commanded the apostles. The apostles heard, they learned, they practiced, and they taught.

Why? Because you and I were nothing without them. We are something because Christ called us, and we are to become something. However, "to become something" means we are to persevere in acquiring knowledge of the truth as it is in Jesus, and by hearing Him and by learning from Him.

Learning Jesus takes time and perseverance. It requires denying oneself, which certainly is not easy. It requires a willingness to accept failure. It requires a realization that we will stumble and fall, that we will fail to do as we should, that we need help, that we cannot do it on our own, and that there is One who will strengthen and support us. He will, but we are to do certain things. We are to take the time and exert the effort. Remember, Jesus called the apostles. After He called them, He instructed them, He tested them, He graded them, He strengthened them, and they went forth in confidence after the resurrection. They learned from Him for more than three years.

How does this apply to us? What are we to do? First, we must realize that the key to the Christian life, or life in Christ, is "learning Christ." There is no other way. Christianity is faith and knowledge. It is not a vague, indefinite, nebulous feeling, experience, or relationship.

We are to acquire the knowledge, and we are to apply it. Our minds are to be enlightened; our understanding is to become clear. The only way to do this is by learning Christ. This is an important point. Because we live in a time that does not like to emphasize this truth. There is too much emphasis on "God is love," and "God loves you!" However, we are to grasp, emphasize, and proclaim that the whole of Christ's life, teachings, death, and resurrection is to convey the love and righteous purposes of God. It cannot be said too often.

Where did the apostles and the authors of the New Testament writings place the emphasis? On Jesus Christ; on learning, hearing, studying, obeying His commands; and on what God has done in Christ. The New Testament emphasizes learning, knowledge, and understanding! Paul writes to Timothy,

> *For this is good and acceptable in the sight of God our Saviour;*
> *Who will* (desires to) *have all men to be saved, and to come unto the knowledge of the truth* [1 Tim. 2:3–4].

We are to come unto a *knowledge of the truth*. The Greek word for *knowledge* in this verse is *epignōsis* and it means "full knowledge," not partial or halfway but full knowledge. We are to have full knowledge of *the truth* as it is in Jesus. That is what we are commanded to do. Not one-half knowledge, not three-quarters knowledge, but full knowledge. What do you think of that?

The Greek word for *truth* in this verse is *alētheia*. What does it mean? Objectively, it means "the reality lying at the basis of an appearance; the manifested veritable essence of a matter." Subjectively, it means "truthfulness, truth, not merely verbal, but sincerity and integrity of character" and "that which is true."

Therefore, we are to acquire full knowledge of the reality, the veritable essence of the matter, the sincerity and integrity of the character and the truth as it is found in Jesus. That is different than just saying *knowledge of the truth*.

Paul says to Timothy that the heart of a right relationship with God is for men and women to acknowledge His truth. "The revelation of Christ in truth must result in the realization of Christ in life," as appropriately expressed by the former missionary to China, Ruth Paxson. Therefore, we are to learn the truth.

Second, we are to think about our relationship to God, really think about it. We are to know about the being, nature, and character of God. We are to begin by seeing the nature of our own being: our weaknesses, our needs, and then our hopelessness and helplessness, and the necessity for a positive relationship to God in Christ.

We are to see Christ as the Messiah, as the One who redeems us, who illuminates our way, who lightens our load, who removes blindness and hardness from our hearts, and as the One who walks with us if we let Him and we will share with Him.

Recall Paul's positive words at the beginning of this fourth chapter: *I THEREFORE, the prisoner of* (in) *the Lord, beseech you that ye walk worthy of the vocation* (calling) *wherewith ye are called* [Eph. 4:1]. Our relationship with Christ is to be such that we walk with Him. Our walk with Christ is to be joyful, uplifting, holy, heavenly, and in obedience to Him. In contrast, the walk without Him is defeating, degrading, and noted for wandering in search of something.

Again, Ruth Paxson regarding walking with Christ, says "[t]he walk in Christ should be as holy and heavenly as the walk in sin was defiling and degrading. So when one leaves the old sphere to enter the new, it involves the decision to renounce the old life in its entirety, and to abandon one's self whole-heartedly to the life of the new."

Third, we are to *Be ready always to give an answer* (a defense) *to every man that asketh you a reason of the hope that is in you* [1 Pet. 3:15]. The Apostle Peter bids the people to be ready to give an answer. He does not say that we are to assert and proclaim certain truths anywhere and everywhere, or to make pronouncements indiscriminately or in every conceivable situation. God endows His people with a spirit of discretion. He wants us to know when and where to speak, and with whom. He wants us to know when to talk and when to be silent, but we are not to deny Him by our actions or by refraining to speak.

Peter is not saying we are to be prepared to solve any and every question that may be raised. Each of us is not required to speak on every subject. However, Peter is reaffirming what Christ taught. We are to make it plain to nonbelievers, to those outside Christ, and to those new to the faith, that we truly worship God and have a strong commitment to walk with Christ.

It is logical that we must have knowledge, learning, understanding, and practical experience. How is this achieved? By the Holy Spirit working within us. Yes, we must open our hearts and minds, but it is the Holy Spirit that produces the fruit. Paul reminds us of this when he tells the Corinthians,

> *But God hath revealed them unto us by his Spirit: for the Spirit searcheth all things, yea, the deep things of God.*
> *For what man knoweth the things of a man, save* (except) *the spirit of man which is in him? even so the things of God knoweth no man, but the Spirit of God* [1 Cor. 2:10–11].

It is the Spirit of God that enables us to know the things that are freely given to us by God.

Paul wants us to know that:

- Christ's teachings in Scripture are understood only through the witness of the Holy Spirit;
- those having the witness of the Holy Spirit have the assurance that it is as strong and firm as if they had actually grasped it in their hands and were clasping it to their breasts; and
- the Spirit of God makes us more positive concerning these truths by increasing our knowledge and understanding, thereby increasing our confidence in His presence, power, and strength.

The truth in Jesus is the most glorious thing we can learn. However, learning this truth does not depend upon a person's natural ability, or intellectual capability, the time or leisure to read or study, the wherewithal to visit certain places or take specific courses, or a person's literacy.

God gives spiritual insight, favor, and understanding to whom He will. This gift cuts across the whole of society and humanity. It does not favor any one group, country, or nationality. It is the Lord through the Holy Spirit that opens the heart and draws people into a positive relationship with Christ. Once the heart has been opened, we are to attend to the things of the Lord. Acts reveals when Lydia's heart was opened by

God, *that she attended* (heed) *unto the things which were spoken of Paul* [Acts 16:14].

If Lydia's heart and mind had not been opened, then the preaching and teaching of Paul would have been mere words. However, God inspired her with reverence for His Word. Consequently, Paul's teachings penetrated her heart and mind, whereas otherwise they would have bounced off dull ears.

We must recognize that it profits us nothing just by hearing the Word. We need the grace of the Holy Spirit to enable us to hear it, to interpret it, and to digest it. When this happens, there is a new confidence instilled in our hearts and minds.

What impact does learning Christ have on a person? By this, I mean learning Him as the apostles proclaim Him and as He taught during His earthly ministry. Why does a person change? Why does a person go from living an unrighteous, evil life to following Christ? We hear of this happening, we see it happen, and we see people change. Why?

Paul tells the Corinthians what some of them had been like, but they had been washed, sanctified, and justified in the name of the Lord Jesus and by the Spirit of God. Why had they changed? Because they had learned something and it was not morality or ethics. They had learned Jesus Christ. Pray God that this will happen in this community and country.

These people learned Christ. What else did they learn? They learned that their sins had been forgiven. Yes, that is true, but there is more. The knowledge that their sins were forgiven was the beginning point, not the end.

It was not a case of saying it does not matter how much we continue to sin or that everything is going to be all right because God is such a loving Father that even if we continue in sin and are disobedient to Him, He will turn the other cheek and continue to shower His love on us.

Those ideas and teachings are not based on Scripture. It is misleading to say that the Gospel is nothing more than an announcement of the forgiveness of sins. To learn Christ is to learn much more than that. The person learning Christ is to learn doctrine, the teachings of Christ. He or she is to have the teachings in their minds, to grab hold of them, and to put them into practice. We, like the Corinthians and Ephesians, are to become more and more conformable to the life of Christ in our thoughts, acts, and deeds. These truths cannot be taught too frequently.

The mere knowledge of Christian doctrine that does not result in a new life is not of Christ.

We need a personal knowledge of the Saviour. As we learn this and experience it, we are to realize it is the objective of all the teachings contained in the Bible. This increasing knowledge of the Lord Jesus is to have a corresponding positive effect upon our conduct and behavior. Its impact is to be the result of knowing Christ, wanting to please Him, wanting to obey His commands, and wanting to walk with Him.

Verse 21 of Chapter 4 begins with the phrase *If so be*. These three words mean "assuming that" or "on the assumption that" you have heard Him and have been taught by Him, *as the truth is in Jesus*. Paul wants to make this phrase simple, so he divides it up. Probably, the best way to consider this verse is to start with: *ye have heard him, have been taught by him, as the truth is in Jesus*. Paul refers to Jesus, not to himself. They are to have learned Christ, not Paul. That is the essence of Paul's words in the following: *But ye have not so learned Christ; If so be that ye have heard him, and have been taught by him, as the truth is in Jesus*.

Why does Paul use the two different names, Christ and Jesus, in referring to the Lord Jesus? Because He is teaching us an important truth. He does not want us to talk or think about some great cosmic Christ who exerts undue influence upon people in this world, nor does he want us to think of salvation in loose or vague terms, or to think of salvation as some idea that is neither practicable nor applicable. The Apostle wants us to think in the terms of something real, something touchable, and something near. Therefore he says *as the truth is in Jesus*. Paul knows we are saved by the person Jesus, not by any other person, way, idea, or philosophy.

John Calvin says regarding Paul's statement, *as the truth is in Jesus* that the Apostle "lays down a twofold knowledge of Christ, one which is true and genuine, and the other counterfeit and spurious. Not that there are really two kinds; but most men falsely persuade themselves that they know Christ, whereas they know nothing but what is carnal. Just as in II Corinthians he says, 'If any man be in Christ let him be a new creature' (II Cor. 5–17), so here he denies that any knowledge of Christ which is not accompanied by mortification of the flesh, is true and sincere."

There is a significant fact about our life in Christ and the Christian faith. What we commonly call Christianity at the beginning of the twenty-first century is composed of several things.

It is the pronouncement of certain facts and events that have taken place, upon which our salvation, or right relationship to God is based. In the fullness of time God sent forth His only begotten Son, made of a woman, made under the law, to redeem us. That Son is Jesus of Nazareth who is essential to our salvation. We are not saved by applying His teachings, but by Jesus Himself. Therefore, we are intimately and inextricably tied to the truth as it is in Jesus.

The Apostle Paul seldom uses the name Jesus by itself in his letters. However, he does in this instance. What is meant by the phrase *as the truth is in Jesus*?

First, the Son of God is the truth. Jesus is the full revelation of God the totality of God's will and promise, the fulfillment of all that is hoped for and commanded, culmination of God's promises. Jesus is different from all others because He is the truth.

Jesus is faithful and obedient, as well as the Mediator and Saviour of all mankind. "He is the presence of power and the radiance of truth in the midst of the world," Markus Barth said.

Second, the Incarnation is the core of the Bible. The deity is revealed in Jesus. The Word, the will, the wisdom of God became incarnate in Jesus, and the Bible stresses the point that He is the man Jesus of Nazareth.

Third, what Jesus taught during His earthly ministry is in reality the essence of the church's doctrine and proclamation. There can be no preaching or teaching unless it is the same as that presented by Jesus. The church, through its preachers and teachers, is to be true to Jesus and His teachings.

Last, *the truth* found in this verse describes conduct that is true and faithful to Jesus and is to be exhibited when walking in His footsteps. Truth in Jesus includes trusting in Jesus, following Jesus, obeying Jesus, and confessing Jesus.

The words *as the truth is in Jesus* are not something only to be said, accepted, known, and believed. That is not sufficient. They are to be practiced at all times. The truth in Jesus is not a part-time or sporadic thing. It is the all time. It is during the good times, bad times, easy times, and hard times. When Peter and John were brought before Annas, the high priest, Caiaphas, and others for healing a lame man and preaching Jesus, they were asked,

> *By what power, or by what name, have ye done this?*

> *Then Peter, filled with the Holy Ghost, said unto them, "Ye rulers of the people, and elders of Israel,*
>
> *Be it known unto you all, . . . that by the name of Jesus Christ of Nazareth, whom ye crucified, whom God raised from the dead, even by him doth this man stand here before you whole.*
>
> *This is* THE STONE WHICH WAS SET AT NOUGHT OF (REJECTED BY) YOU BUILDERS, WHICH IS BECOME THE HEAD OF THE CORNER (CHIEF CORNERSTONE).
>
> *Neither is there salvation in any other: for there is none other name under heaven given among men, whereby we must be saved* [Acts 4:7–8, 10–12].

The truth is in Jesus. Our Lord Himself says, *I am the way, the truth, and the life: no man cometh unto the Father, but by me* [John 14:6].

That is why the Apostle says to the Ephesians, *Ye were, Ye are, Ye are to become*. Because you have so learned Christ, and you have acquired a knowledge of the truth in Jesus.

We cannot separate the doctrine we have learned or will learn from Jesus of Nazareth. We cannot remain or become, which ever is the case, academic, or theoretical, or detached when it comes to Jesus Christ. We cannot forget that salvation comes in a Person and that Person is Jesus. God forbid that we should do any of these things.

This reminds me of an experience at the First Presbyterian Church in Pittsburgh while participating in a Bible study class. It was an in-depth study that progressed during twelve weeks from milk and soft foods to tough meat. The course focused on the Lord Jesus Christ and His teachings.

There was a lady in the group who was obviously struggling and having difficulty learning Christ and the truth as it is in Him. This went on for a number of weeks. She was what you may describe as a nominal Christian. One night near the end of the class after a certain amount of discussion, the Holy Spirit enlightened her, and she exclaimed, "Now I know and understand that Jesus is My Lord and My God!"

We are to hear Him, we are to learn Him, and we are to know individually that He is my Lord and my God!

Amen!

7

God's Amazing Grace

> *That ye put off concerning the former conversation the old man, which is corrupt according to the deceitful lusts;*
> *And be renewed in the spirit of your mind;*
> *And that ye put on the new man, which after God is created in righteousness and true holiness* [Eph. 4:22–24].

"Amazing Grace" is a favorite hymn of many Christians and has been for many years. The music is delightful, and the words are meaningful. We have been noting the contrasts contained in Paul's letter to the Ephesians, which helps us gain a better understanding of our relationship to the Lord Jesus Christ and the difference between being in Christ and outside Christ.

"Amazing Grace" contains significant contrasts, which is one of the reasons we thoroughly enjoy it. Think on the contrasts in John Newton's beloved hymn:

> *God's amazing grace,*
> *a wretch like me;*
> *Once was lost,*
> *now am found;*
> *Was blind,*
> *now I see;*
> *Grace taught my heart to fear,*
> *grace my fear relieved;*
> *Through many dangers, toils, and snares,*
> *'Tis grace hath brought me safe thus far.*

These contrasts are appealing and convey the truth of our relationship to Christ as members of His body.

The Scripture being considered contains contrasts: *put off, put on; old man, new man; corrupt, renewed; deceitful lusts, righteousness* and *true Holiness*. Hopefully, these truths will be appealing, enabling us to better understand our relationship to Christ and to see more clearly God's amazing grace.

These three verses offer constructive thoughts. Since the truth is in Christ, these verses are a vital link tying together the truth in previous verses [Eph. 4:17–21], and the definitive descriptions presented in the following verses [Eph. 4:25–32]. They are most important in learning Christ, hearing Him, and being taught by Him. They describe what our conduct should be as members of Christ's body. They are the lynchpin between what precedes this Scripture and what follows.

These verses [Eph. 4:22–24] are important theologically, especially with respect to the Doctrine of Sanctification. They impart a true understanding of the New Testament teaching of holiness and of the practical aspects of applying it to our daily living. Paul emphasizes tying certain things together and showing the contrasts between the life in Christ and life outside Him.

There are two important factors in these three verses. First, consider God's part and our part regarding sanctification. It is not all God's doing, whereby we are merely passive vessels waiting to be turned on or turned around. These verses are "the crossroads between God's sovereign work through grace and man's cooperative action through faith," as Ruth Paxson explains it. These verses exhort us to practical holiness in every phase of our lives.

Paul points to the source of life in two different spheres. The old man is corrupt in deceitful lusts, and the new man is created in righteousness and true holiness. In this comparison, he shows that the character of life depends upon its source and determines its conduct. Life in the old man goes back to its source and produces corrupt conduct. Life in the new man goes back to its source and produces righteous and holy conduct.

What does the verb *corrupt* mean? The Greek word is *phtheirō*. It signifies "to destroy by bringing a person into a worse state." It also incorporates into its meaning the effect of evil company upon the manners of believers and the effect of associating with those denying the truth and holding to false doctrines as they travel on the morally decaying road to final ruin.

In contrast, the Greek word for *created* is *ktizō*. It signifies "to create, but always as an act of God," whether it be a natural creation or a spiritual creation.

What is Paul saying in these three verses? He is presenting a negative and saying that we are to *put off the old man*, but we are not to stop at that point. We are to take a positive step and *put on the new man*. We are not to remain naked, nor are we to be like a baby and wait for someone to change us or to dress us.

When considering these truths presented by Paul, it is important to note what he is saying and the urgency with which he is speaking. When Paul said *put off*, he was literally saying put away, get rid of it, don't ever get it out and put it on again. He was speaking with finality.

When the Apostle says *put on* he is saying "to clothe" oneself. He is saying, *To make* (create) *in himself of twain* (the two) *one new man* [Eph. 2:15]. The *one new man* is Christ's partner. Paul says *The inner man* [Eph. 3:16] is Christ dwelling in the heart of the believer, and he is to *put on the new man, which after God is created in righteousness and true holiness* [Eph. 4:24]. The *new man* is to be clothed and created by God, not by the natural man.

There is a point we are not to overlook when considering what we are to *put off* and to *put on*. These two commands are part and parcel of the sentence beginning with verse 20 and proceeding through verse 24 that says,

> . . . *as the truth is in Jesus:* . . .
> *ye put off* . . . *the old man, which is corrupt according to the deceitful lusts;*
> . . . *And that ye put on the new man, which after God is created in righteousness and true holiness* [Eph. 4:21–22, 24].

The putting off and the putting on describe an external action that is accompanied and complemented by an internal development. The change within a person is reflected by a change on the outside.

When the person is freed from the shackles of the old man, he or she receives and wears the attire of a new person. These clothing metaphors indicate a change of heart and mind as well as an invisible appearance. The dressing on the outside reflects the change on the inside.

We have all heard the saying, "Clothes make the man." A person's garments and the act of changing them are effective symbols. They can tell much about a person, and they can also exhibit a person's status, position, authority, or power. Assuming a different mantle can result in a person exercising more authority or responsibility and can even result in changing his or her personality. Investing a person with a new robe or uniform conveys receiving and assuming a new office with a different status. Further, it should make that person realize the public responsibility he has assumed.

What is a person to do when this happens? Each of us is to become new. We are to present our bodies as a living sacrifice. We are to be transformed by the will of our minds. We are to learn the will of God by experience, knowledge, and prayer.

Putting on and putting off is a result of being renewed in one's mind and spirit. There needs to be a marked change on the inside as well as the outside. When this happens, the renewed mind and the newly dressed body are to be used in serving God and walking with Jesus.

It is God's creative power that renews a person at the very nucleus of his or her being. Scripture states the situation in a two-fold manner: what man is and needs and what he or she has been given to do. A person is not meant to be a lazy, passive spectator, nor to be merely the object or tool of some destiny. A person is to actively participate in this confrontation between the old and the new with his or her insight, emotion, and will. He or she is a partner in the struggle, and must take sides and cooperate. The putting on and putting off affirm an event and state the objectives.

> *Therefore if any man be in Christ, he is a new creature* (creation): *old things are passed away; behold, all things are become new.*
> *And all things are of God, who hath reconciled us to himself by Jesus Christ, and hath given to us the ministry of reconciliation;*
> *To wit* (That is), *that God was in Christ, reconciling the world unto himself, not imputing their trespasses unto them; and hath committed unto us the word of reconciliation* [2 Cor. 5:17–19].

This teaching says, "If any man desires to obtain a place in Christ, that is, in His kingdom or His church, let him be a new creature." No one is to glory in any ability, achievement, or distinction that he or she may have since the primary commendation of a true believer is to deny himself.

The old things of which the Apostle speaks are those which have not been reformed by the Spirit of God and are fading away. It is only the new man, the new creature, who can flower and increase in the kingdom of God.

When the Apostle says, *All things are of God*, what does he mean? All things belong to Christ's kingdom. "If we wish to be Christ's, we must be regenerated by God, but this is no ordinary gift," John Calvin says.

In this context, the Apostle is speaking of the grace of regeneration that God confers upon His elect as the Creator of the church. In so doing, He refashions them into His own image. This truth should humble us and make us realize what thanks and gratitude we are to give to God, who has made us into new creatures.

It is God who reconciles us, who creates within us the new creature. When examining this point, we must understand its two parts: man's reconciliation with God and the means by which we obtain the benefits of that reconciliation.

The whole Gospel is directed toward these two conditions offered by God. Paul admonishes the Corinthians because they had not distinguished between the true and false prophets and did not know what they should look for in an apostle. Further, they did not know Christ's teachings as they should.

Therefore, the Apostle endeavors to: stir them into action; motivate them to learn more about Christ and His teachings; and make progress as new creatures in Christ.

Paul wants the Corinthians to know that the grace of reconciliation is made available so that they may share in it. It is not withheld. It is given, and they are to put it on. "Man's reconciliation by God's grace is inseparable from God's confidence and command that man 'be reconciled,'" as pronounced by the renowned theologian Markus Barth. Think of that: God's confidence and command that we be reconciled.

When considering these truths, bear in mind that Paul means reconciliation is not taken from something that resides within a person or has been lying dormant since natural birth. Rather, it is something that comes from the outside, something that enters into a person and makes him a new creature.

Possibly we may obtain a clearer insight regarding putting off the old and putting on the new by examining the parable that Jesus told after casting out a devil and what was to replace it. Jesus said,

> *When the unclean spirit is gone out of a man, . . . he saith, I will return unto my house whence I came out.*

> *Then goeth he, and taketh to* (with) *him seven other spirits more wicked than himself; and the last state of that man is worse than the first* [Luke 11:24, 26].

When the evil spirit goes out of a person, something needs to replace it. The space cannot remain void because then other evil spirits, worse than the first, can enter in. When this happens the condition can be much worse than it was originally. Putting off the old man can be dangerous, if we are not at the same time putting on the new man. The two events go together: *put off* the old; and *put on* the new. These two actions are to be performed once and for all.

However, this does not mean the new person in Christ will live a life of ease and be free from all its challenges and torments. Putting off the old does not eliminate opposition, temptations, tests, tribulations, and unpleasantness. Recall what the Lord Jesus encountered during His earthly ministry. He was reviled, opposed, challenged, mocked, tested, and tempted. He did not have a life of ease, but one of glory.

When we *put on* the new person, we will embrace the commands and teachings of Christ. They will provide light for our pathway and the strength to overcome adversity and the temptations of Satan, the evil one. The new person will be renewed daily in the spirit of his or her mind by the Holy Spirit. He will always be with them and never cease to help them. Thank God! This continuous support is important to understanding the Doctrine of Sanctification.

Remember, the Apostle says, *That ye put off concerning the former conversation* (conduct) *the old man* [Eph. 4:22]. The word *conversation* in this verse means the "tenor of life," or "conduct, behavior, mode or manner of living." It includes all our actions. On the other hand, the Apostle writes to the Philippians and says, *Only let your conversation be as it becometh* (conduct be worthy of) *the gospel of Christ* [Phil. 1:27]. By this he means "let your life be" as it becomes the Gospel. It cannot be half one or half another. It must be one or the other.

What does he mean by putting off *the former conversation* of the old man? He means the whole personality. Why does he say *old* in writing to the Ephesians? He is contrasting something that used to be true of the Ephesians in their former life, but it was not to be true of them in their present life, nor should it be in the future.

He tells the Ephesians that they are to *put off* the old. They are to be what they are. They may forget, they may relapse, but they are to remember what they are by the grace of God.

We are to recognize and remember what Paul says to the Romans, *Knowing this, that our old man is crucified with him* [Rom. 6:6]. By God's sovereign act the old man was crucified with Christ. The "old man" died on the Cross, just as Christ did. God put an end to the "old man" and replaced it with the new creature in Christ. The old man is gone, the new one has arrived.

Putting on the new man requires our intelligent, wholehearted co-operation and willingness in putting off the old. We have a responsibility in all this and we are to fulfill it.

What responsibilities are we to perform in putting off the old man? First, it requires an act of faith. We are to see the old man where God sees him, on the Cross crucified with Christ. Our faith is to function in such a way that we will see the old man where grace has placed him. This is the first step in our walk of practical holiness;

Second, Chapter 6 in Romans reveals that we have been taken out of our old position in sin and in the flesh. However, there is an important point to note. Although God's power delivers us from sin and its power, it does not deliver us from sin's presence. That is an important distinction. Even though we *put off the old man*, the temptations of the flesh and mind are still present, and they continue to tempt us and always will.

Consequently, there are two natures present within us: one that yields to the evil one, the enticements of the world, and the temptations of the flesh and mind, and the other that chooses to live under the Lordship of Jesus Christ, according to the divine calling, and under the control of the Holy Spirit. The two natures require self-examination, discovering where and how we are walking and with whom, determining who is controlling the flesh and mind, and praying to God that our thoughts, conduct, and behavior are worthy of the new man.

Third, we are to abandon the old life, reject it, ignore it, turn from it, and cast it away. We are to realize that it can appear in our character, conduct, ethical attitudes and actions, and in the compromises we make for expediency's sake.

When putting on the new man we are to renounce the former manner of living. Paul said to the Colossians,

> *Lie not one to another, seeing that ye have put off the old man with his deeds;*
> *And have put on the new man, which is renewed in knowledge after the image of him that created him* [Col. 3:9–10].

The Apostle says that the "new man is constantly being renewed or developed until he attains a knowledge of the God who (re)created him. The more a believer knows and understands of God, the more he will be like God in character and conduct," as enunciated in the King James Study Bible.

Although we say that putting off the old man is a one time action, we don't mean that we will never have to do it again. When a person becomes a member of Christ's body, he or she *puts off* the old and *puts on* the new. But the old has a habit of reappearing again and again. Even in our new self, we sometimes reach for what we once thought was comfortable, familiar, and pleasurable.

The Apostle exhorts the Colossians to do what? *Put off the old man with his deeds* and *Put on the new man, which is renewed in knowledge after the image of him that created him* [Col. 3:9–10]. *The old man* is what we are by nature, and *the new man* is one who is reformed by the Spirit of Christ. We are reformed to the spirit of righteousness through the power of the Holy Spirit and by responding obediently. It is through Christ we obtain that which renews us, and it is not perishable.

The Apostle says, *renewed in knowledge*. The knowledge of which he speaks is full knowledge received through the illumination of the Holy Spirit. This process enlightens a person with the truth and transforms him at the same time. He or she is renewed after the image of God, which resides in the soul. It is the reason that one is upright, and it enables one to exhibit wisdom, righteousness, and goodness. It is the image of God that enables us to aspire to the highest perfection and blessedness.

Then the Apostle proceeds to show that there are no divisions where *Christ is all, and in all* [Col. 3:11]. Christ is the beginning and the end. It is through Him that we receive spiritual righteousness. Therefore, Paul tells the Colossians that they are to *put on the new man* as God's elect or chosen ones. Calvin says, with clarity, an important theological truth stating, "This can be paraphrased to say, God has chosen you to Himself, has sanctified you, and received you unto His love on the condition that you shall be merciful." To this the Apostle adds, you shall

> *Put on therefore, as the elect* (chosen) *of God, . . . kindness, humbleness of mind, meekness, long-suffering;*
> *Forbearing* (Bearing with) *one another, and forgiving one another, . . .* [Col. 3:12–13].

Remember, we are chosen and called to be something. Therefore, Paul describes what we are to be and commands us to strive for what Christ wants us to become. If we don't become these things, knowing we are beloved of God and counted among the community of believers, we are only fooling ourselves.

The Apostle does not stop there. He says,

> *And above all these things put on charity, which is the bond of perfectness.*
> *And let the peace of God rule in your hearts, to the which also ye are called in one body; and be ye thankful.*
> *Let the word of Christ dwell in you richly in all wisdom; teaching and admonishing one another in psalms and hymns and spiritual songs, singing with grace in your hearts to the Lord* [Col. 3:14–16].

We are to be all these things in the name of the Lord Jesus while giving thanks to God the Father.

Jesus' encounter with the Pharisees who were challenging Him is relevant to putting off and putting on.

> *And he spake also a parable unto them; No man putteth a piece of a new garment upon an old; if otherwise, then both the new maketh a rent* (tear), *and the piece that was taken out of the new agreeth not* (does not match) *with the old.*
> *And no man putteth new wine into old bottles* (wineskins); *else the new wine will burst the bottles, and be spilled, and the bottles shall perish* (be ruined).
> *But new wine must be put into new bottles* (wineskins); *and both are preserved.*
> *No man also having drunk old wine straightway desireth new: for he saith, The old is better* [Luke 5:36–39].

New wine must be put into new wineskins. When it is, both are preserved. Jesus' preaching and teaching, His Gospel, and His presence are the new life he offers to His followers. It is a new life; it is not patchwork, nor is it a combination that in essence is a dilution. The people of Jesus' day knew the danger of putting new wine into old wineskins.

The new wine is Jesus Himself, nothing less. We are to be new wineskins that contain "the dynamic, fermentive, life changing power of His gospel," according to the respected author, pastor, and preacher, Lloyd Ogilvie. New wineskins need to be elastic, flexible, and adjustable so they can contain the teachings of Jesus.

We don't want to put old wine in new wineskins. Why? Because it just sits there. We are to be new wineskins for the new wine of Jesus every day. We are to be elastic so we can expand to hold the richness and fullness of the new wine; we are to be flexible so that the new wine can ferment within us so that we can be used as He would use us; and we are to be adjustable so we can meet the demands and requirements placed upon us. We are called to *put off the old* and to *put on the new*. We are to be constantly aware of this. We should remind ourselves of it daily. We should remember each day God's amazing grace and the contrasts between being in Christ and outside Christ. We must remind ourselves every day that our external appearance and internal condition are to reflect the new man; that we are to actively participate, we are not passive vessels; that we are to *put off* and to *put on*; that we are to be new wineskins everyday, for the new wine which is Jesus; and that we are called to become something, by God's grace.

Amen!

8

Corrupt Through the Lusts of Deceit

That ye put off concerning the former conversation (conduct)
the old man, which is corrupt according to the deceitful lusts;
And be renewed in the spirit of your mind;
And that ye put on the new man, which after God is created in righteousness and true holiness [Eph. 4:22–24].

Why are we to learn the teachings of Christ through Paul? Why are we to *put off the old man* and *put on the new*? We are to do this because it will bring us and keep us in a right relationship with God and His Son, Jesus Christ. It will enable us to have life and to have it more abundantly.

Remember, within every saint there are two natures: one that yields to the instigations of the Evil One, and the one that desires to live under the reign of Christ, according to His calling, His teachings, and His commands. Paul exhorts us to *put off* and to *put on* because he understands the two natures present within us and realizes the importance of choosing the life that is to have mastery over us.

Although we make the right choice, we must recognize it requires examining ourselves daily and asking, are we yielding to the influence of the Evil One and the pleasures, pursuits, and plans of the world? Are we being dominated by the nature of man in our attitudes, acts, desires, deeds, conversation, and conduct? We are not to allow this self-appraisal to degenerate into morbid self-introspection, which impairs honest self-judgment, when honest self-judgment is to be exercised according to Christ's teachings.

The God and Father of our Lord Jesus Christ, which is blessed for evermore, knoweth that I lie not [2 Cor. 11:31].

Corrupt Through the Lusts of Deceit 69

> *But if we walk in the light, as he is in the light, we have fellowship one with another, and the blood of Jesus Christ cleanseth us from all sin* [1 John 1:7].

The Apostle John conveys several thoughts in this particular verse. It is a definite sign of our union with God when we are conformed to Him. However, one point should be crystal clear: it is not the purity of our daily living that reconciles us to God. It is when God's purity shines in us that our unity with Him is assured. Of course, it must be stated and acknowledged that whenever God's holiness fills us, there is no room for filth, uncleanliness, and darkness. We cannot live properly unless we cleave to God. Our fellowship is to be with God, not just with one another.

A person who is not controlled by a positive awe of and respect for God, who does not endeavor to devote himself or herself to God, and who does not seek to walk in the light does not *put off* the old and *put on* the new. The people sincerely seeking to serve and worship God in every aspect of their lives may be regarded as walking in the light even though they may err, stumble, and fall due to the burdens experienced, or the weaknesses of the flesh.

This particular verse [1 John 1:7], teaches that the bond of our union with God is the blood of Jesus Christ, and from this comes the fruit by which our sins are forgiven and we are cleansed. The Atonement of Christ cultivates within the unrighteous person a righteous heart. The remission of sins is tied inextricably to repentance.

God's grace that freely pardons our sins is not given just once and only once. It is offered to believers each and every day. Hopefully, we agree that we need God's forgiveness on a daily basis, and thank God He provides it.

John's statement says *from all sin*. Though we are guilty on many counts and have many faults, God forgives us, and through His forgiveness we become pleasing to Him when we repent. Consequently, our sins do not prevent us from pleasing Him since we have been cleansed by the blood of Christ. It is the cleansing power of Christ's blood that makes us acceptable to God. We should be thankful that God's grace, love, and forgiveness are available to us each and every day.

With these thoughts in mind, we turn our attention to corruption, lusts, and deceit. Remember, our examination begins by saying, *But ye have not so learned Christ* and continues by saying, *That ye put off con-*

cerning . . . *the old man, which is corrupt according to the deceitful lusts* [Eph. 4:20–22]. Paul says that everything about the life and person of Jesus teaches us that we are to *put off the old man* and leave the life of sin. What we learn from Christ should help us do just that. Christ provides not only the teaching and the direction, but through the Holy Spirit the power. We are to be cleansed because we are temples of the living God.

The Apostle prepares us step by step as he instructs us, strives to increase our knowledge and understanding, and exhorts us to live as Christ would have us to live.

What does Paul say about *deceitful lusts* or the lusts of deceit? The Greek word for "lust" is *epithumia* and it means an "over desire" or a "strong desire of any kind." The meaning of "lust" as derived from the Greek is not necessarily base and immoral. However, it is evil if it is inconsistent with the will of God.

Our Lord says, *With desire* (I have earnestly desired) *to eat this passover with you before I suffer* [Luke 22:15]. The word for *desire* is basically the same word as the one used for "lust." In Luke, it is used for a positive statement, whereas in Ephesians it is used in a negative sense.

Lust has come to mean something that is almost exclusively and entirely a negative. Why is that so, when you consider our Master used the word in a positive and beautiful way? Could the reason be that people, by their nature, are overpowered by evil desires? Therefore, an "over desire" or "strong desire" has become associated with the things of the flesh and not with the things of the mind and the spirit. Once again man takes something of God that is pure and good, and dilutes or perverts it.

Paul says the old man is *corrupt according to deceitful lusts*, or probably a better translation is "corrupt as a result of the lusts of deceit." This leads one to ask, what about the natural instincts with which God has endowed man, such as hunger, sex, self-defense, and others? These instincts are not bad, they are good if they are of God. They have been given to us for the enjoyment and preservation of life. They were instilled within man for good, not for evil.

Christ is the Head of the body, and we are members of His body. Therefore, we are under His control and are to obey Him according to God's will. There is a definite analogy to the instincts God has given us. They are part and parcel of our body, but they are to be subject to the control of our minds and are to be exercised in obedience to God's will.

God gave us a mind, a brain, a conscience, and a spirit. Man's conscience and spirit are to be controlled by God, and in turn man's mind is to be enlightened; he is to acquire knowledge and understanding. Therefore, we are to use our brains to control our bodies and the instincts that dwell therein. There is nothing wrong with the instincts within us. To say there is, is to deny Scripture.

However, it is equally true to say that our instincts must be in the right place; they must be governed, controlled, and ordered by the mind (and understanding) according to the will of God and the teachings of Christ. The tragedy is that the nature of man has allowed the order to get out of control and the instincts to gain the upper hand. When this happens, there are disruptions and eventually chaos. The evil lusts take charge. This is true whether it is an isolated instance, the handling of a situation, or the living of a life.

When evil lusts gain control, most of the troubles occur with which we are acquainted or to which we have been exposed. This means the ones that we normally bring to mind, as well as the ones enumerated by Paul in verses 25–32 of this chapter. All of them are the result, in the final analysis, of evil lusts. Think how this affects individuals, marriages, families, work environments, churches, communities, and nations.

Evil desires gain control when positive reasoning and the understanding of Christ's teachings and God's will are either ignored or utterly abandoned

By allowing his instincts to gain control, man in his sin makes a mess of things. Man is not to be controlled by his instincts; he is to be controlled by God and to be obedient to His commands and teachings.

The *old man* is corrupt as a result of the lusts of deceit. When a person is corrupt, he is decaying. Paul says that deceit manipulates the lusts, and in turn, the lusts manipulate the man. The Greek word for *deceit* which the Apostle uses is *apate*. It means "lusts excited by deceit, of which deceit is the source of strength for the lust." It is not that the lusts or desires are deceitful in themselves, but that deceit triggers the lust.

Please note and remember that Paul, under the influence of the Holy Spirit, correctly uses the word "deceit." Bear in mind that deceit is one of the great characteristics of life in this world. We need to be aware of it.

What should we consider regarding deceit?

> NOW *the serpent was more subtile* (cunning) *than any beast of the field* [Gen. 3:1].
>
> *But I fear, lest by any means, as the serpent beguiled* (deceived) *Eve through his subtilty* (craftiness), *so your minds should be corrupted from the simplicity that is in Christ* [2 Cor. 11:3].
>
> Jesus says, *Ye are of your father the devil, and the lusts* (desires) *of your father ye will do. He was a murderer from the beginning, and abode* (stands) *not in the truth, because there is no truth in him. When he speaketh a lie, he speaketh of* (from) *his own* (nature)*: for he is a liar, and the father of it* [John 8:44].

This is how Scripture and our Lord speak of deceit.

Peter and the other apostles knew that deceit was a dreadful problem. They knew that the saints to whom they were writing were confronted by three major impediments hindering their growth in the faith and serving Christ as His disciples. They are the secular world, false preaching and teaching, and the unrelenting attacks of Satan. These factors have a negative impact upon our behavior and produce dire consequences.

Peter provides an excellent description regarding what happens when individuals succumb to false teachers, damnable heresies, and destructive ways. The result is that they

- *Speak evil of the things that they understand not;*
- *Shall utterly perish in their own corruption;*
- *Shall receive the reward* (wages) *of unrighteousness;*
- (Are) *sporting themselves with* (reveling in) *their own deceivings;*
- (Are) *having eyes full of adultery;*
- *Cannot cease from sin;*
- (Are) *beguiling* (enticing) *unstable souls;*
- (Have) *a heart . . . exercised* (trained) *with covetous practices;* (and)
- (Become) *cursed children.*

[Selections from 2 Pet. 2:12–14].

These are the results. Can you picture it? Can you think of situations where you have seen or heard of such conditions and actions?

Peter continues by describing what that type of life consists of, because they

- *Have forsaken the right way;*
- *Loved the wages of unrighteousness;*
- (Were) *rebuked for his* (their) *iniquity;*
- (Are) *wells without water;*
- (Are) *clouds . . . carried with a tempest;*
- *Allure through the lusts of the flesh, through much wantonness* (licentiousness);
- *Are the servants of corruption; and*
- (Are) *brought in* (into) *bondage.*

[Selections from 2 Pet. 2:15–19].

Guess what had been promised to all those who succumbed and accepted that life? *Freedom. That was what was promised!* What actually happened?

> *They themselves became servants* (slaves) *of corruption: for of whom a man is overcome, of the same is he brought in* (into) *bondage. The latter end is worse with them than the beginning* [2 Pet. 2:19–20].

Members of the early church said, and some preachers and teachers today say, you do not have to believe all that the apostles taught. It is too strict. It is too confining. It does not apply to our particular circumstances or to our situation. This has been the story of *the father of lies* and his children from the beginning.

When deceit comes, it enters into a person and hardens him or her. It comes in a nice, attractive package, it is tempting, it is enticing, but it hardens one's heart. The author of the Letter to the Hebrews exhorts us not to harden our hearts, and he urges us to exhort one another on a daily basis.

> *HARDEN NOT YOUR HEARTS, AS IN THE PROVOCATION* (REBELLION), *IN THE DAY OF TEMPTATION* (TRIAL) *IN THE WILDERNESS* [Heb. 3:8].

> *But exhort one another daily, while it is called TODAY; lest any of you be hardened through the deceitfulness of sin* [Heb. 3:13].

> *While it is said, Today if ye will hear his voice, harden not your hearts, as in the provocation* (rebellion) [Heb. 3:15].
>
> *Again, he limiteth* (designates) *a certain day, saying in David, TODAY, after so long a time; as it is said, TODAY IF YE WILL HEAR HIS VOICE, HARDEN NOT YOUR HEARTS* [Heb. 4:7].

Note the emphasis on *Today*. We are not to let one day go by that hardens our hearts! Not one day! Have you ever thought of it that way: not one day? Not for even one day are we to let our hearts harden!

Sin is deceitful! It hardens a person! Think of what Jeremiah says, *The heart is deceitful above all things, and desperately wicked* (incurably sick)*: who can know it* [Jer. 17:9]? Man does not know it. It fools him constantly.

Sin is deceitful! How does it deceive? First, it always flatters us. It appeals to our egos, to our pride, to our self-centeredness, and to building us up while tearing others down. It preys on the vanity of our minds by exalting our being, position, status, and power. This has been true since the time of Adam and Eve.

It always comes with a smile and in a manner that is attractive for the particular moment or occasion. It always says do it this way rather than what God would have us to do.

Second, sin always discourages thought or meditation. Sin and deceit always want to play upon feelings, desires, and emotions.

Why is this so? Because if a mind blessed with understanding by the Holy Spirit begins to function, it chases sin and does not allow it to operate. Proper thinking discourages sin. Conversely, sin discourages thought and that is part of deceit's strategy. This is the pattern of deceit. This is the way it operates.

Third, deceit always presents plausible arguments. Why not do something? It is only natural; everyone is doing it. What difference does it make? Who else will know? Go ahead, express yourself. When deceit does this, it does certain other things: it conceals certain facts and factors; it hides or colors the difference between right and wrong; it prevents moral categories or codes from being considered; it obliterates our view of God, His Son, and Their teachings; and it obscures the consequences of sinful action.

Fourth, deceit waves the banner of motives, but, alas, they are false motives. They will appeal to acquiring knowledge by enticing you to read bad or untruthful books or articles. They will distort basic truths by saying everyone is reading it, or experiencing it, or enjoying it.

Deceit will seek to subdue someone by appealing to their proper motives with false information. Consequently, people who set out to help someone or some worthy cause end up taking the wrong road and impairing the truth as found in Jesus Christ. We have to beware of *deceitful lusts*.

Fifth and finally, sin and deceit always offer the one thing they can never give—satisfaction!

Sin working through lust never gives, it always takes away. Think of the Prodigal Son. He left with everything, he returned with nothing.

Sin and *deceitful lusts* rob us mentally, physically, spiritually, morally, and in every positive respect. "It robs us of character, integrity, chastity, purity, honesty, morality, uprightness, balance, sensitivity, delicacy, and everything noble in a person," as truthfully stated by Martyn Lloyd-Jones.

No wonder the Apostle says, *Put off . . . the old man, which is corrupt according to the deceitful lusts.*

Amen!

9

The Power of God

> *That ye put off concerning the former conversation the old man, which is corrupt according to the deceitful lusts;*
> *And be renewed in the spirit of your mind;*
> *And that ye put on the new man, which after God is created in righteousness and true holiness* [Eph. 4:22–24].

The Apostle Paul proceeds in an orderly manner. He takes one step at a time, he builds one brick upon another.

The first three chapters of this Epistle describe and present the centrality of Christ and the grace of God. Paul wants the Ephesians to know

- that they were called into the kingdom of God, through God's wonderful mercy that shines forth in the salvation that flows freely from Him;
- that he prayed for them (us) to be enlightened in the full knowledge of Christ, through the riches of God's grace;
- the wretchedness of their being and nature before they were called to be *in Christ*; thanks to God's grace and kindness;
- that they were aliens from the promises of eternal life;
- that he had been appointed an apostle to the Gentiles, so they might be engrafted into the body of Christ; and
- that they are to be grateful for the ministry presented to them and the truths of Christ contained in these teachings.

At the end of the third chapter, Paul prays for the Ephesians

> . . . to be strengthened with might by his Spirit in the inner man;
> That Christ dwell in your hearts by faith; That ye . . .
> May be able to comprehend (understand);
> And to know the love of Christ; That ye might be filled with all the fullness of God;
> According to the power that worketh in us [Eph. 3:16–20].

The Apostle stresses unity in Christ in chapter 4 verses 1–16. Then he turns personal and practical saying we are not to walk as other Gentiles walk in darkness, ignorance, and blindness, and we are not to give ourselves over to lasciviousness, uncleanness, and greediness.

Paul amplifies upon his commands by saying, *But ye have not so learned Christ* [Eph. 4:20] or, more accurately, you have not learned *in Christ*. We are members of Christ's body. If we have heard Paul and been taught by him, we are to focus on what he stresses throughout the balance of this letter. He does not focus on these things until he has set the stage and put numerous teachings in place. He begins this portion of Scripture by saying, *put off . . . the old man,* (and) *put on the new man* [Eph. 4:22, 24].

The Apostle does not command us to do these things until after he has revealed the centrality of Christ, prayed that we will be strengthened by the power of the Spirit within us, prayed that we will comprehend, prayed for the ability to work within us, and stated emphatically what we have not learned, and what we should have learned *in Christ*.

What is Scripture saying regarding *put off . . . the old man,* (and) *put on the new man*? Before proceeding to discuss this question, it is important to keep in mind to whom Paul is speaking. He is speaking to those: who are in Christ; who have received and accepted the gift of Christ; who recognize they are the branches, and He is the vine; who realize they are to renew themselves by deepening or expanding their knowledge and understanding; and who commit themselves to an intimate relationship with Christ. It is only with this understanding and within these boundaries that we can proceed to examine that question.

The putting off of the old man is something we have to do, but it can be done only if we are in Christ and He is in us. The command is given to those members of His body, who have the power and ability, are in unity with Christ, have learned in Christ, have heard Him, and have been taught by Him *as the truth is in Jesus*. This command is not for everyone, and it does not apply to everyone.

The command is in the present tense. It calls us to action. It will always be in the present tense. It does not call us to pray about it. Remember, the Apostle prayed for strength in the inner man, as well as for the power, might, and ability that Christ provides. Therefore, we are to pray for these things.

Please note a fine line of delineation. There comes a time when, as members of Christ's body, we are to act and not just sit back and say we are going to pray because it is out of our hands, or we will do something when God sends us a postcard, or a thunderbolt, or new clothes; then we will do something.

Do not misunderstand. We are to pray. It is a most important part of our relationship with God and Christ. But it is not something we are to hide behind, do glibly, or say, "Oh well, let's take it to the Lord in prayer."

There are times in our positive relationship when we are to act as long as the basis of our action is in Christ. Paul has laid the groundwork, he has established the relationship, now it is time to act and to get on with it.

Recall the woman who had an issue of blood for twelve years. She touched the hem of Christ's garment. The woman had faith; she believed. She knew He had the strength, power, and ability to bless her. Behold, she acted, and she received.

Remember, He has the power! The New Testament teaching is explicit. If we are commanded to do something, then we should proceed with full confidence that the Lord has the power and the will for us to do it. Why? Because we are members of His body and we are in Christ.

There is a point to make at this stage: some people pray out of fear, others just want to pray about something, thinking it will go away. They think that they can be delivered if they remain completely passive, and that God does not act with power. They ignore the New Testament teachings. There comes a time when you have to do more than pray. You have to think in Christ. You have to apply the knowledge, understanding, and teachings as they are found in Jesus.

We are witnesses. We are to be good ones, not bad ones, or even worse, we are not to be nothing witnesses. We are to learn Scripture, to think about it, and to apply it. Scripture illuminates us, and the Holy

Spirit enlightens us. However, we are to act, we are to do, and we are to have confidence in the power available within the context described.

The devil, or evil one, in his deceitful, subtle way may encourage us to pray in a blind and unintelligent manner, because he knows that if we don't apply Scripture, if we don't think about what we have heard and have been taught as the truth is in Jesus, then we will not act as we should.

You have heard it stated many times, "Take it to the Lord and leave it with Him" or "Let go and let God." Some say it is quite simple; just do that and go merrily on your way and everything will be A-OK. Further, the Lord will bestow upon you some wonderful deliverance and your actual relationship to Christ does not make any difference.

"This false teaching has been propagated for many years. Some have tried to practice it, but they have not been delivered from their troubles," as proclaimed by Martyn Lloyd-Jones, nor have they experienced an intimate relationship with Christ. What needs to happen is to *put on the new man* and this can happen only in Christ. The "Let go and let God" teaching is not scriptural. Why would I say that when it has become widely accepted in some circles?

"If it were true, then the Apostle did not have to write that portion of Ephesians which begins with the seventeenth verse of the fourth chapter and goes to the end of the chapter," to quote and paraphrase Lloyd-Jones. Paul would not have said,

- *Put off* (and) *put on;*
- *Putting away lying;*
- *BE YE ANGRY AND SIN NOT;*
- *Steal no more;*
- *Let no corrupt communication proceed out of your mouth;*
- *Let all bitterness, wrath, anger, clamor, and evil speaking be put away; and*
- *Be ye kind one to another.*

[Selections from Eph. 4:22, 24, 26, 28, 29, 31, 32]

If you bypass Scripture, then you deny it.

When considering the last two and one-half chapters of Ephesians it is almost natural for someone to raise a question about justification.

Some say you receive your sanctification and justification in the same way by faith. However, there is a difference. According to Martyn Lloyd-Jones: "Justification is entirely by faith, and it is given when a person has no real spiritual life or ability." Otto Weber says, "Justification is a completed reality. [It] meets man as a person." Sanctification involves the actions of the individual as a member of the body of Christ. The person "is the one acting; he produces good works; he loves; he is thankful," as Otto Weber said. Sanctification is possible only by constantly renewing the power within as it is received from Christ, learning how we should act, and having the willingness to do so.

For we are his workmanship (creation), *created in Christ Jesus unto* (for) *good works* [Eph. 2:10]. We are his workmanship! We cannot do anything until He makes us new. But when He does, we can do things. We can *put off* and we can *put on*. Once we are new creatures in Him, then we can perform. That is why the Apostle commands us and exhorts us to obey His commands and teachings.

God never commands us to do anything without providing the wherewithal to do it. Thus, St. Augustine prayed: "Give what you command, and command what you will." When we become new creatures with the spirit of God and Christ in us and the Holy Spirit functioning, then we realize the power is there. When this happens and we recognize it, then we can act.

How are we to act? What are we to do? We have to remind ourselves who we are and what we are. We are branches of the vine; we are not what we were. We should start our day by saying we are new creatures, the old one has passed away. We are to be new wineskins for the new wine every day. We are to remember Christ's teachings, and that the truth is in Him.

We are to recognize the nature and character of the old life and remember the description of it contained in Scripture. Note how the Apostle keeps reminding us of the former life. He does not want us going back to it. He wants us to be rid of it. If we are in Christ, we will be new creatures.

We are to impress upon ourselves the utter inconsistency of claiming to be members of the body of Christ but continuing to live the old way. We are not to be hypocrites. We are not to say one thing and then do another. As members of Christ's body we are not to claim to be one thing and then act in another way. Our conduct and behavior are to be that of the new man, not the old one. We are to grasp what Paul says,

> *Only let your conversation* (or action as a citizen, or member) *be as it becometh* (conduct be worthy of) *the gospel of Christ* [Phil. 1:27].

The message is clear. Does our behavior becometh the Gospel of Christ? Does our behavior reflect our inner being and commitment? Our conversation, conduct, and behavior are to be according to the Gospel of Christ.

The external actions are to exhibit the indwelling Christ and the power of the Holy Spirit. People are changed when they become members of the body of Christ. Probably one of the more famous instances is that of Chuck Colson. He was involved in the Watergate break-in during the Nixon years, convicted, and sent to prison. While there he was converted by the saving grace of Jesus Christ. He became an effective witness to both those in and out of prison.

There is another true story to share with you that Martyn Lloyd-Jones told.

> "An ordinary sort of person lived an evil and dissolute life given to drinking, fighting, a foul temper, and out of control when drunk. He was known for his flamboyant mustache. He took great pride in it. He did not darken the steps of the church.
>
> Then the unexpected happened: he went to Church, he was converted, he accepted Jesus as His Lord and Saviour, he attended church on Sundays and Wednesday nights with his very noticeable mustache, which had been the center of his pride and the primary cause of his troubles. One Sunday he appeared in Church without his mustaches. He had previously referred to them in the plural due to their size. As he left the sanctuary the minister asked if someone had made a remark about his mustache or had offended him or what had happened? He responded saying he had looked in the mirror and saw his two mustaches, recognized what they represented and said, "them things don't belong to a Christian!" So he cut them and shaved them off.

Oh, that we could cut off the mustaches of our thoughts, our ideas, our attitudes, and our actions that do not belong to a true Christian.

Oh, that we would accept Jesus in such a way that we would allow His power to work within and give us the ability to do as He would have us to do. Oh, that we can *put off the old man* and all "Them things that don't belong to a Christian."

The Apostle says, *And have no fellowship with the unfruitful works of darkness, but rather reprove* (expose) *them* [Eph. 5:11]. In other words, have nothing to do with the works of darkness. Have no discussion, have nothing to do with sin. Don't be like Eve; don't even begin to talk with her.

Paul tells the Romans to

> *Cast off the works of darkness, and let us put on the armor of light.*
> *. . . put ye on the Lord Jesus Christ, and make not provision for the flesh, to fulfill the lusts thereof* [Rom. 13:12, 14]

The Apostle tells the Romans two things: *put ye on the Lord Jesus Christ, and make not provision for the flesh*. This metaphor occurs frequently in Scripture. "To put on Christ means here to be defended on every side by the power of His Spirit, and thus rendered fit to discharge all the duties of holiness," as faithfully expressed by John Calvin. It is in this manner that the image of God is renewed within us.

When God adopts us, He engrafts us into the body of His only-begotten Son with this requirement that we *put off* our former life and *put on* the new life in Christ. Further, as long as we carry our flesh with us, which is throughout our journey on earth, we cannot ignore it or neglect it.

In so doing, we are to be concerned with our desires and our conduct. It has been stated that nature is content with that which is required to sustain it, but the appetites of man are insatiable. Paul reminds us that we are to provide for the needs of the flesh; however, we are not to indulge our lustful desires. Therefore, when we *make not provision for the flesh*, we are not to feed the old man that is in us; we are not to lead or push ourselves into temptation. There are places we should not go, things we should not do. The old man is to be *put off*, along with all the factors, large and small, that marred his being and his relationship with the Lord Jesus.

This admonition applies to people, to bad influences, to reading material, to shows, to anything that feeds the old man. Job says,

> *I made a covenant with mine eyes; . . .*
> *If my step hath turned out of the way, and mine heart walked after mine eyes, . . .*
> *Then let me sow, and let another eat; yea, let my offspring* (harvest) *be rooted* (uprooted) *out* [Job 31:1, 7–8]

Solomon says in Proverbs, *Let thine eyes look right on, and let thine eyelids look straight before thee* [Prov. 4:25]. If something entices us, then we are to turn from it, no matter what it may be.

Lastly, in addition to not making provision for the flesh, we are told to mortify the flesh. Paul says to the Romans, *For if ye live after the flesh, ye shall die: but if ye through the Spirit do mortify* (put to death) *the deeds of the body, ye shall live* [Rom. 8:13].

The Apostle exhorts the followers based upon doctrine. We are to renounce the carnal desires and devote ourselves to the righteousness of God. It is our obligation to do so. If we do not, we are fighting against God.

Those who *live after the flesh* may boast of justification by faith, but they are doing so without the Spirit of Christ. Further, where there is no confidence in God, then there is no love of righteousness.

Everyone who is justified in Christ through God's mercy is called to live a life worthy of that vocation. The believers are to embrace Him, the person Jesus, not only for their justification but for their sanctification.

Therefore, Paul says, *through the Spirit mortify* (put to death) *the deeds of the body*. This does not mean to literally destroy the body, but it does mean to subdue the lusts; put to death the *deceitful lusts* or deeds of the old man; attack, starve, eliminate those actions, thoughts, ideas which do not belong to, nor are part of the body of Christ; and eliminate "them things [that] don't belong to a Christian!" The Apostle goes further, saying, *But I keep under* (discipline) *my body, and bring it into subjection* [1 Cor. 9:27].

Paul is saying, according to John Calvin, "My life ought to provide some sort of example to others. Therefore, I take pains to live in such a way that my character and conduct do not conflict with what I teach (or profess), and that I may not, therefore, neglect the very things which I demand of others (or myself) so involving myself in great disgrace and causing serious offence to my brothers (and sisters)."

We are called to do, to act, and to be *as the truth is in Jesus* [Eph. 4:21]. We are to *put off . . . the old man* (and) *put on the new man* [Eph.

4:22, 24]. May our eyes be open to Scripture. May God grant us honesty. May we realize the Spirit of God is within us. May we have confidence that God through Christ gives us the might, power, and ability to do, to be, and to become, as He would have us to become.

Amen!

10

Controlled by the Spirit of Christ

And be renewed in the spirit of your mind [Eph. 4:23].

We should thank God continually for Paul's amazing mind, but more importantly for the impact of the Holy Spirit upon Paul as he wrote, preached, taught, and lived.

The Scripture being considered is relevant to *put off . . . the old man* (and) *put on the new man* [Eph. 4:22, 24].

Luke records in Acts,

> *AND Saul, yet breathing out threatenings and slaughter* (murder) *against the disciples of the Lord, went unto the high priest* [Acts 9:1].
>
> *Then Ananias answered, Lord, I have heard by many of this man, how much evil* (harm) *he hath done to thy saints at Jerusalem* [Acts 9:13].

Then Luke reveals that Ananias obeyed Jesus, went to the house where Paul was, and told Paul that Jesus had sent him, that he might receive his sight and be filled with the Holy Spirit.

Ananias told Saul the reason he visited him was, *that thou mightest receive thy sight, and be filled with the Holy Ghost*. After Ananias had spoken these words, *immediately there fell from his* (Paul's) *eyes as it had been* (something like) *scales: and he received sight forthwith* (at once), *and arose, and was baptized* [Acts 9:17-18]. After Paul had eaten and was strengthened, he spent certain days with the disciples at Damascus.

Acts reveals the astounding change in Paul, the contrast in him, when it says, *And straightway he preached Christ in the synagogues, that he is the Son of God* [Acts 9:20].

Look what happened in the matter of a few days. He went from *breathing out threatenings and slaughter against the disciples* to preaching Christ as the Son of God. What a profound change!

Is it any wonder that Paul tells the Ephesians (and us) to *put off* the old and to *put on* the new? When considering this teaching, we cannot overlook the connecting link, which is *And be renewed in the spirit of your mind* [Eph. 4:23].

Recall Paul's amazing experience in preparing to go to Damascus, traveling to Damascus, waiting in Damascus, preaching in Damascus, and leaving Damascus.

What we are doing or should be doing is analogous to Paul setting out for Damascus and then seeing what happened to him. We start on our journey with our own mindsets, ideas, and experiences; we travel with our own convictions, toward our own objectives; we may have to wait to receive the real food, or the understanding, or the knowledge, or we may become impatient because we do not proceed more rapidly; and when we receive it we should be strengthened, and we should be filled.

Remember, Paul received his sight, was filled with the Holy Spirit, and was strengthened for the tasks appointed to him. What tasks were appointed him? He was a chosen vessel, and he was to bear Jesus' name to the Gentiles, kings, and the children of Israel. What was to happen to him? Jesus said, *For I will show him how great things he must suffer for my name's sake* [Acts 9:16].

Finally, we are to do something here and now. Note that Paul began to preach Jesus as the Son of God right there in Damascus. He did not wait after he had received Christ's command. He went straightway, immediately, at once. We are to receive; be filled; eat the meat, even the tough meat; we are to be strengthened; and we are to witness.

There are situations existing in congregations, communities, schools, clubs, the world, and even families that can only be handled in the manner described in the ninth chapter of Acts.

What is required to bring about a change, to *put off* the old and *put on* the new?

First, look at what the Master says,

> *If ye love me, keep my commandments.*
> *And I will pray the Father, and he shall give you another Comforter* (Helper), *that he may abide with you forever;*

> *Even the Sprit of truth; whom the world cannot receive, . . . but ye know him; for he dwelleth with you, and shall be in you.*
> *I will not leave you comfortless* (orphans)*: I will come to you* [John 14:15–18].

If we really love Jesus, we will at least try to keep His commandments. People have many thoughts and opinions about love. This is especially true about the love of Christ. However, true love of Christ is really determined by keeping His teachings and being obedient unto Him. This is the unique rule. We should realize that our affections and emotions can be sinful and our love for Christ at fault unless it exhibits and expresses true obedience to Him. Thy will be done! Yet we cannot show pure obedience unless we know Him, His teachings, and the truth that is in Him. This cannot be accomplished without the Holy Spirit filling us, without hearing and learning the truth as it is in Jesus.

Note, Jesus says *Even the Spirit of truth* in referring to the Comforter. Christ says that the Holy Spirit is the teacher of truth. We are to be taught inwardly by Him, otherwise our minds are held captive by vanity and falsehood.

In these verses, Jesus exhorts His disciples not to be puffed up and not to rely on their pride and reasoning, for they cannot know Him unless the Holy Spirit operates within them and fills them. "Christ's words show that nothing relating to the Holy Spirit can be learned from human reason, but that He is known only by the experience in faith," as John Calvin acknowledges through the revelation provided by the Holy Spirit. We know Him because the Spirit dwells within us. If the Spirit does not dwell within us then we will not know Him.

Paul continues by saying, *I will not leave you comfortless* (orphans). "This passage teaches what men are and can do without the protection of the Spirit. They are orphans, exposed to every sort of trickery and injustice, unequal to governing themselves, . . . unfit to do anything of themselves. The only remedy for such a great weakness is for Christ to rule us by His Spirit, which he promises to do. First, . . . the disciples are reminded of their weakness, that they may distrust themselves and rely on the protection of Christ. Secondly, He promises them a remedy . . . for he says He will never leave them. . . . He shows the manner in which He dwells in His people and fills all things—by the power of His Spirit. It is therefore clear that the grace of the Spirit is a striking testimony to His divinity," as beautifully described by John Calvin

Again Jesus stresses the importance of keeping His commandments, keeping His words. He says,

> *If a man love me, he will keep my words: and my Father will love him, and we will come unto him, and make our abode* (home) *with him* [John 14:23].

When Jesus says *will keep my words,* he means "keeping My sayings, statements, and teachings." Why did He say this? To exhort His disciples, His followers, to the earnest study of godliness. Why? So that we might make greater progress in faith and in the truth as it is in Jesus. We are to study, make the effort, become knowledgeable, and understand Christ's words.

This is what Jesus taught; this is what the New Testament expounds. This is the mark that distinguishes those following the teachings of the Gospel from those who do not. Oh, yes, we hear all the excuses: the people will not come, the course is too hard or too easy, or the time is too early or too late. And there are many more excuses.

However, as members of Christ's body we are to follow His teachings. We are not to remain in the comfort zone, or we will be outside the body of Christ.

Christ commands us to keep His teachings and to apply ourselves to godliness. How can this be done if we do not study His words and seek to apply them? This is how we show our love to Him.

Jesus calls us His friends and says we are no longer servants. He opens His heart and mind to us. He says in a kind, friendly way, I have explained to you the secrets of heavenly wisdom and a right relationship with God the Father, and I am sharing with you the things I have learned from our Father.

What is our reaction when a friend reveals to us a truth that will have a beneficial impact upon us? We want more. Christ is supplying us with an inexhaustible supply of riches, which are found in the Gospel. The Gospel opens Christ's heart and mind so that it is revealed to us. It is not to be doubted nor obscured. It is to be opened fully. Therefore, we are to partake of it as the early believers did.

The second thing is to *be renewed in the spirit of your mind.* What does this mean? Renewal means more than to be reformed or reoriented or reactivated. The spirit and mind can exert a powerful effect upon a person. Therefore, a renewed spirit and mind means a total change in the whole person. The internal and external capabilities are affected and impacted.

Put off . . . the old man (and) *put on the new*. Paul tells us in verse 22 that we are to *put off*, and in verse 24 he says, *put on*. Notice how he connects these two verses whereby he calls us to action. The strong link connecting them is *be renewed in the spirit of your mind*.

The Greek word for *renewed* is *ananeoō*. The way it is used does not mean that the mind, in its powers of memory, judgment, and perception, is to be renewed, but that *the spirit of your mind* under the controlling power of the Holy Spirit is to be renewed. It is to direct its interests and energies toward God, it is to enjoy fellowship with the Father and the Son, and it is to fulfill the will of God. That is how we are to be renewed.

It is interesting to note a subtle difference in these verses. Paul calls us to action, to *put off* and to *put on*. But he specifically says, *be renewed*. This is stated in a passive sense. It is not something we do, it is done to us, it happens to us. We are to be renewed or made new again. It is the work of the Holy Spirit functioning within us. Actually, this phrase should be interpreted "go on being renewed." It is a continuous process. The renewing is the work of the Holy Spirit. However, we are not to do anything to hinder or impede the process.

If we are to *put off* the old and *put on* the new, the third thing required is to hear God. We are to be united with Christ, then we will hear God. What hinders us from hearing Him is being taken up with other things. Therefore, we are to cultivate the hearing process with respect to the Lord Jesus Christ and God the Father. If we have other priorities we cannot hear Him.

When we *put off the old man* and *put on the new man*, we are to be renewed in the spirit of the mind. There are certain thoughts to consider when examining and digesting this portion of Christ's teaching: the Apostle speaks of the spirit of the mind. He is not talking about the spirit and mind, nor is he speaking about the body, soul, and spirit. "Paul is directing his statements to that principle within us that guides, controls, governs, and operates the mind itself. In addition to our intellect and faculties, there is a spirit of the mind that controls the workings of the mind" as stated by Martyn Lloyd-Jones. It directs the abilities of the mind and has the power to control the direction of the mind.

When studying these things, I have to chuckle and laugh. These thoughts certainly put to rest the idea that once you accept Christ and become a member of His body, you can let your mind go to sleep and accept everything by faith. That is a fallacious idea that should be replaced by the truths expressed in Scripture.

Much of the New Testament was written almost two thousand years ago to people who did not have the educational benefits we know and expect. Yet the Gospel confirms profound truths. We are to grapple with it and to understand it. Pray God that we will continuously be renewed in the spirit of the mind so we can grow as members of Christ's body.

The word *renewed* should automatically turn our attention to the third chapter of Genesis. We need to be renewed. "There is nothing more important to understand than the Doctrine of the Fall, man in sin; it is the key to the whole Bible!!" according to Martyn Lloyd-Jones' insight.

A person cannot really accept the Doctrine of Salvation unless he or she knows something about the Fall of Man. That is one primary reason we need both the Old Testament and the New Testament.

Man fell, he was no longer in a right relationship with God, and as a consequence the spirit of his mind went wrong. The spirit of the mind came under the control of the flesh, the nature of man, and Satan. As a result the whole outlook was in the wrong direction. A person's thinking and reasoning became twisted, perverted, and polluted.

No wonder Paul says between *put off* and *put on* that you are to *be renewed in the spirit of your mind*. The trouble with people, with individuals, is not their minds. Their minds can function and perform very capably. The problem is in the spirit of the mind, that power which governs and controls the mind.

Why emphasize *be renewed in the spirit of your mind*? Paul tells the Romans how they are to yield themselves, saying, *For as ye have yielded* (presented) *your members servants* (slaves) *to uncleanness and to iniquity* (lawlessness) *unto iniquity; even so now yield* (present) *your members servants* (slaves) *to righteousness unto holiness* [Rom. 6:19].

Paul tells them that they are to turn from practicing sin to practicing holiness. The Apostle informs the Romans that there is, as Calvin was to say later, "No greater absurdity, and indeed no greater dishonor or shame than that the spiritual grace of Christ should have less influence over them than earthly freedom." The Apostle says when you compare sin and righteousness there should be much greater enthusiasm for serving righteousness than being obedient to sin. Paul exhorts them to obey righteousness with much greater determination than to be the servants of sin.

Paul tells the Corinthians that *the natural man receiveth not the things of the Spirit of God* [1 Cor. 2:14]. He does not say he lacks the intellect, and he does not say he lacks the capability. But he does say that they do not receive *the things of the Spirit of God* because *they are foolishness unto him.* That is a significant difference.

It is the spirit of the mind that is wrong, not the mind as an organ or an instrument. There are people with excellent minds and fine brainpower, but they do not accept Christ. It is the spirit of their minds that is wrong. Earlier in Ephesians the Apostle says,

> Who were dead in trespasses and sins,
> *Wherein in time past ye walked according to the course* (age) *of this world, according to the prince of the power of the air, the spirit that now worketh in the children of disobedience* [Eph. 2:1–2].

Then there is that direct, wonderful statement by Paul,

> *For they that are after the flesh do mind* (set their minds on) *the things of the flesh; but they that are after the Spirit the things of the Spirit.*
> *For to be carnally minded is death; but to be spiritually minded is life and peace.*
> *Because the carnal mind is enmity against God: for it is not subject to the law of God, neither indeed can* (it) *be.*
> *So then they that are in the flesh cannot please God*
> [Rom. 8:5–8].

Scripture reveals in no uncertain terms that *the spirit of the mind* has gone astray and needs to *be renewed.*

What is to be done when the mind goes astray? The person needs to be regenerated. He or she needs to be renewed. The mind needs to be enlightened. It is the Holy Spirit that leads us to life. The Holy Spirit guides and governs the spirit of the mind. It is the activity of the Spirit of God within us that leads to our blessedness.

When a person is renewed it does not mean his faculties have been changed. One still has the same mental capacities, but he is receiving new directions and abiding by them. Paul still had the same mind and capabilities after his encounter on the road to Damascus and receiving his sight. However, he had been filled with the Holy Ghost, and the spirit of his mind had been renewed. He was governed in an entirely new way. His mind had been enlightened.

What happened to Paul and what happens to us when we are continuously renewed in the spirit of our minds? Paul put into practice an intelligent change. He did not act in a mechanical way. He spent time with the disciples, he studied, he practiced.

Paul had been set right and went forth in new directions, not in the old ways. The spirit of his mind was changed and all of his brilliance and capabilities were guided by this new power within him. The Apostle did not proceed to do things blindly, because he had been told to do something. He learned, and he used his intelligence. We are to do the same.

Next the Apostle changed inwardly; after this, it was exhibited by his outward conduct. The Spirit of Christ works from the inside out, not from the outside in.

Paul had been enlightened. He had knowledge of his faith in Christ in his heart and mind. After Jesus called him, he felt compelled to be in a right relationship with God. The spirit of his mind had been renewed.

The Apostle did not just change his moral behavior nor his opinion about a few things or certain items, nor did he acquire a new interest or hobby. No, that is not what happened. He was changed in the spirit of his mind. He did not become mild-mannered. He remained the same hard-charging person he had been, but with a new Lord.

What does this mean? Paul was consumed, governed, captivated, and controlled by the Spirit of Christ directing his mind and his interests. He still had the same mind and intellect. He was still a tent maker, but he had been renewed. The spirit of the mind is to be renewed.

If the spirit of the mind is continuously renewed, then like Paul we shall *put off the old man* and *put on* the new. Then as this happens, we shall apply, act, and practice as members of Christ's body. Because the spirit of the mind is being controlled and governed as it should be. *For as he thinketh in his heart, so is he* [Prov. 23:7].

Therefore, *be controlled by the Spirit of Christ.*
Amen!

11

Created in Righteousness

And that ye put on the new man, which after God is created in righteousness and true holiness [Eph. 4:24].

The twenty-fourth verse of this fourth chapter is magnificent! It contains a command, but it also describes the context in which this command is to be carried out. It establishes specific boundaries. Look at the primary points in this verse: . . . *that ye* (that means you and me); *put on the new man* (all the old is to be cast off); *which after God,* (according to God) *is created in righteousness and true holiness.*

When considering the whole verse you realize much more is involved than just putting on the new man. It is to be done in a certain way. The Greek word for *created* is *ktizō*. It means "create," but it always means creating as an act of God, whether it is a natural creation or a spiritual creation. In this verse, it means a spiritual creation.

Scripture says, *which after God is created,* or more accurately "according to God" *is created.* This means it is something that did not exist previously. There was not a spark or ember burning just waiting to be fanned into a burning fire. There was nothing there. There was not some divine nature residing in a person waiting to be ignited.

The new man is the product of a spiritual birth. He is created, he does not evolve. He is not a product of some self-culture, he is an outright creation of God. *Created* means "to make something out of nothing." Therefore, it may read, *that ye put on the new man,* (according to God), *created in righteousness and true holiness.*

The person in Christ, receives two commandments, *put off* the old, *put on* the new. We have to be aware of the negatives, the things from which we are to stay away, and the things we are not to do. On the other hand, we are to be equally aware of the new, what we are to *put on*, what we are to do. We are commanded to do two things: *put off, put on.*

Paul in his second letter to the Corinthians admonishes them to do certain things and to refrain from others. He begins by saying,

> *WE then, as workers together with him . . . receive not the grace of God in vain [2 Cor. 6:1].*
>
>> *Giving no offense in any thing, that the ministry be not blamed: But in all things approving* (commending) *ourselves as the ministers of God, in much patience* (endurance), *in afflictions, in necessities, in distresses* [2 Cor. 6:3–4].

Then Paul continues to demonstrate what they are to do and not to do. He addresses the following to the Corinthian believers:

> *They are to work together as Christ's ambassadors and ministers of His Gospel. They are to labor to have the Gospel's message prevail in their daily living by exhibiting it in their attitude and conduct. They are to exhort others so that their mission will be effective. The Gospel's teachings are to be accompanied by continuous exhortations to obey and to practice His commands.*

They were to give no occasion for stumbling or offense. Paul's three points when exhorting the Corinthian saints, plus all the members of Christ's body, are to show the characteristics that should be evident in the ministers of the Gospel in any and all circumstances, show that they possess these qualities, and warn the Corinthians not to recognize people as Christ's servants who do not behave according to the example He gave them. They are not to hinder the progress of the Gospel by exhibiting faults which cause others to stumble. He may be addressing this primarily to the ministers, but it applies to all the members of Christ's body.

Next, the Apostle exhorts the followers to show much patience. He points out that he has been spared no trial in order to prove the faithfulness of his ministry. Note all the things he lists after saying *approving* (commending) *ourselves as the ministers of God: in much patience* (endurance), *in afflictions, in necessities, in distresses, in stripes, in imprisonments, in tumults, in labors, in watchings* (sleeplessness), and *in fastings* [2 Cor. 6:4–5].

He continues, saying,

> *By pureness, by knowledge, by long-suffering, by kindness, by the Holy Ghost, by love unfeigned* (without hypocrisy),

> *By the word of truth, by the power of God, by the armor of righteousness* [2 Cor. 6:6–7].

Note the change. He proceeds from pureness, knowledge, long-suffering, and kindness, which we may want to attribute to ourselves, but Paul says it is *by the Holy Ghost*, which we cannot attribute to ourselves. He follows by citing other things that are not inherent characteristics of man: *love unfeigned* (without hypocrisy), . . . *word of truth*, . . . *power of God, by the armor of righteousness!*

Further, Paul says we are to prove ourselves by overcoming our circumstances, trials, and tribulations through the Holy Spirit as he compares positive traits with negative ones:

> *By honor and dishonor, by evil report and good report: as deceivers, and yet true;*
> *As unknown, and yet well known; as dying, and behold, we live; as chastened, and not killed;*
> *As sorrowful, yet always rejoicing; as poor, yet making many rich; as having nothing, and yet possessing all things* [2 Cor. 6:8–10].

These contrasts emphasize what the follower is to *put on* and what he is to discard. The Apostle denotes the characteristics our conduct is to exhibit regardless of what may beset or befall us, including attacks, insults, and innuendos being hurled at us.

When attacked by evil men or, more significantly, by those claiming membership in Christ's church, we are to walk uprightly and not be diverted by the unkindnesses of other people. If we are, then it proves that we have not looked to God alone. When Paul was exposed to infamy, insults, and attacks he did not give in to them but continued to focus on God and His will. Paul continues by saying that his mouth is open to them, and his heart is enlarged. By this he means his mouth is opened to them because his heart is enlarged. He exhorts them to enlarge their hearts.

He reminds them that they are not to be yoked to unbelievers and they are not to have fellowship with them. We are not to have fellowship with them in their pollutions. Though we may have to associate with nonbelievers in certain situations, we are to avoid them when we can, and our fellowship is to be with believers.

Paul says there is no agreement between idols and the temple of God. Scripture is rather explicit about this. It is sacrilegious to introduce or allow an idol or idolatrous worship into God's temple.

How does this apply to us? We are the true temples of God, and He dwells within us. The only way God can dwell among us is to dwell in us. He has promised to dwell in the midst of us.

God has promised to *walk among you, and will be your God, and ye shall be my people* [Lev. 26:12]. "From God's promise to dwell among us we may infer that He also remains in us," as appropriately described by John Calvin. The symbol of God's dwelling with His people in the Old Testament was the ark. The symbol of the ark in the Old Testament finds its fulfillment in Jesus and under His reign.

The Apostle says, *Wherefore COME OUT FROM AMONG THEM, AND BE YE SEPARATE, saith the Lord* [2 Cor. 6:17]. This exhortation refers back to Isaiah,

> *AWAKE, awake; put on thy strength, O Zion; put on thy beautiful garments, O Jerusalem, the holy city: for henceforth there shall no more come into thee the uncircumcised and the unclean* [Isa. 52:1].

The prophet warns the people to take care because the vessels used in divine worship had been entrusted to them. They are to guard against pollutions and are not to be infected by them. This applies today. If we are God's vessels and He dwells among us, then we are to keep ourselves undefiled so that God's dwelling place will not be infected and polluted. We are to avoid and steer clear of all uncleanness and not participate in it. This requires knowledge and obedience.

Paul concludes these instructions by saying,

> *... AND I WILL RECEIVE YOU,*
> *AND WILL BE A FATHER UNTO YOU, AND YE SHALL BE*
> *MY SONS AND DAUGHTERS, saith the Lord Almighty*
> [2 Cor. 6:17–18].

We are members of God's family. How many times have we heard people say, "Remember the family honor, conduct yourself like a member of the family, don't do anything to disgrace the family, act like your mother or father." These and similar exhortations are repeated each and every day.

Since God is our Father, we are to conduct ourselves with a zeal for holiness and a desire to obey His commands. It is an affront to God to call Him Father and then to behave in an unclean and impure way.

> *HAVING therefore these promises, dearly beloved, let us cleanse ourselves from all filthiness of the flesh and spirit, perfecting holiness in the fear of God* [2 Cor. 7:1].

This beautiful statement flows from the preceding truths. It is explicitly stated with clarity and full force that

> *Having . . . these promises;*
> *let us cleanse ourselves*
> *from all filthiness of flesh and spirit,*
> *perfecting holiness*
> *in the fear of God.*

God freely bestows His promises upon us and elicits gratitude in return.

In Genesis, God appeared unto Abram and said, *I am the Almighty God* (I am thy God), but He adds to that statement a very important command: *walk before me, and be thou perfect* (blameless) [Gen. 17:1]. This part of the statement is often overlooked. But it should not be!

Paul says that this condition is part of God's promises. If it is not explicit, then it is implicit. It is part and parcel of God's promises and the process of sanctification to which we have been summoned. Bearing these thoughts in mind let us continue examining *put on the new man, which after God is created in righteousness and true holiness*. It is only natural to ask a few questions before proceeding:

- What is the new man?
- What is the new creation in a person?
- What is it that God creates and puts into us?
- What do the believers receive?
- How does righteousness, holiness, and truth impact upon a believer?
- What is more important than realizing God dwells among us and in us?
- What is to be the character and nature of the new life, new person, new creation?

These questions require our utmost attention.

The first half of Ephesians concentrates on doctrine, while the second half applies Christ's teachings and is directed toward the behavior and conduct of the followers in the Way. Paul, in verses 22–24, emphasizes in an acceptable and understandable way the practical aspects of what God has done in redemption and regeneration.

How do we *put on the new man*? According to God it is created in righteousness and true holiness. This is in direct contrast to the old man, which is corrupt according to the lusts of deceit. Therefore, it is important to have a proper understanding of the terms righteousness, holiness, and truth, as used in *And that ye put on the new man, which after God is created in righteousness and true holiness.*

The Greek word for *righteousness* is *dikaiosunē*. It means "rightness, justice." It is the quality of being right or just. It signifies the attributes of God which show His faithfulness, truthfulness, purity, and holiness. These characteristics are consistent with His own nature and promises; He is not indifferent to sin, nor does He regard sin lightly. He expresses His righteousness by condemning sin.

This Greek word is found in the following sayings of Christ: whatever is right or just and conforms to the revealed will of God [Matt. 5:6, 10, 20; John 16:8, 10]; whatever has been appointed by God is to be acknowledged and obeyed [Matt. 3:15, 21:32]; the sum total of God's requirements [Matt. 6:33]; and man's spiritual duties and responsibilities to his neighbors, to God, and to self [Matt. 6:1, 2, 4, 5–15,16–18]. Also, the preaching of the apostles and the writings of the New Testament authors, under the influence of Holy Spirit, emphasize God's righteousness and His righteous dealing with sin and sinners through Christ's death on the Cross.

Righteousness is to exhibit itself in righteous action. Those who believe on the Lord Jesus Christ and seek to obey Him realize His commands are offered in order to bring us into a right relationship with God the Father. The person trusting in Christ has the righteousness of God that is in Christ within himself [2 Cor. 5:21]. When we are in Christ, we become all that God requires of us, all that we can never be on our own.

Abraham obtained righteousness from God because he accepted the Word of God, responded by that act of the mind and spirit called faith, and submitted himself to God's control. As a result, God accepted Abraham as one who had fulfilled all His requirements. Thus, faith properly exercised brings a person into a vital union with God in Christ and inevitably produces righteous living in *conformity to the will of God.*

Righteousness means being obedient to the will of God by exercising through faith, as Abraham did, the right ordering, right understanding, right living, and right relationships. It means accepting Christ as their leader and becoming a knowledgeable follower.

The second term to consider is *holiness*. The Greek word used in this verse is *hosiotes*. It means "that quality of holiness which is manifested in those who have regard (respect, esteem) equally to grace and truth." It is recognized in those receiving grace and truth through the Lord Jesus Christ. Further, it involves a right relationship with God. This particular word *hosiotes* is used twice in Scripture and in both instances in conjunction with the word meaning *righteousness*.

This word has a slightly different meaning than the other Greek words interpreted by the English word "holiness." In this instance, the emphasis is upon having the right relationship with God, not upon:

- Sanctification (*hagiasmos*)—separation to God, set apart to God;
- Personal conduct (*hagiosune*)—the absolute holiness of Christ during His life in the flesh, or perfecting holiness in the fear of God, or unblamable in the person of Christ; and
- An abstract quality of holiness (*hagiotes*)—which was manifested in the conduct of Paul and his fellow laborers."

Holiness in the new man reflects an essential characteristic of God. It is something we cannot describe adequately. It is ineffable! God is holy! And He is eternally different from sin and evil in its essence and manifestation.

The Apostle tells us that righteousness and holiness are two characteristics the new man is to *put on*. When reading this verse you should note it says, *And that ye put on the new man, which after God is created in righteousness and true holiness.* Read it again, and it says the same thing.

We have examined the lynchpin in detail. We are to

- *put off the old man*;
- "get rid of them things that don't belong to a Christian";
- eliminate and overcome *the deceitful lusts*;
- *be renewed in the spirit of your mind*, which means being changed. (Remember Saul on the way to Damascus and Paul the Apostle afterwards);
- be created according to God to make something out of nothing; and then
- *put on the new man* in *righteousness and true holiness.*

Since we have considered these truths it is proper to proceed to the next verse and concentrate on those that follow, right? Wrong!

Some scholars say this verse should be translated "which after God is created in righteousness and holiness of the truth." The Greek word for *truth* is *alētheia* and it is the same word that is used in the verse that says *as the truth is in Jesus*. The meaning in these two verses is the same. It is not merely ethical truth, but truth in all its fullness and scope as embodied in Christ. Jesus was and is the perfect expression of truth.

Alētheia is exactly the same word used by Jesus when He said, *I am the way, the truth, and the life* [John 14:6]. Also, the same Greek word is used in the following verses:

> *Then said Jesus to those Jews which believed on him, If ye continue (abide) in my word, then are ye my disciples indeed;*
> *And ye shall know the truth, and the truth shall make you free* [John 8:31–32].

These words of our Master are often misquoted and just as frequently misinterpreted. What does He say, what is the condition? Abide in my word, be my disciples, then you shall know the truth, and you shall be free. You do not know the truth nor do you become free if you do not continue in His Word and remain His disciple.

We are to persevere in the faith. There are many who profess to be His disciples, but they are not, and as Calvin says, they "do not deserve to be accounted as such." Jesus makes it plain and direct that we are to strive sincerely and earnestly after the truth that is in Him. He will enlighten and illuminate us. Remember, remember, and remember, we are to *put on the new man, which after God is created in righteousness and true holiness.*

Amen!

12

Truth According to God

> *And that ye put on the new man, which after God is created in righteousness and true holiness* [Eph. 4:24].

The following words of the Lord Jesus Christ should not only command our attention but serve as a guiding light as we seek to *walk worthy of the vocation* (calling) *wherewith ye are called* [Eph. 4:1].

> *If ye continue* (abide) *in my word,...*
> *... ye shall know the truth, and the truth shall make you free* [John 8:31–32].

This particular statement about truth is that which God has revealed about Himself in the Lord Jesus Christ. The freedom about which He speaks is not freedom to do and act as one may choose, nor is it complete freedom of thought and conscience. It is more important. It is freedom from sin, from the power and control of sin. The truth in these two verses is to know God, to know the Lord Jesus Christ, and to respond in a positive, obedient manner.

Why is there an emphasis on *the truth* in the words of the Lord Jesus? It may be enlightening to reflect upon what the Old Testament has to say about truth. This should enable us to see the positive fulfillment of it in our Lord and Master. Truth in the Old Testament is a quality properly belonging to God. *O Lord God of truth* [Ps. 31:5]. This is repeated in other psalms.

This revelation that truth is an inherent quality in God's self is expressed in its being a quality of His activity.

> *Before the Lord: for he cometh, for he cometh to judge the earth: he shall judge the world with righteousness, and the people with his truth* [Ps. 96:13].

And it is listed with other qualities of God.

> *For thy mercy* (loving kindness) *is great above the heavens* (skies)*: and thy truth reacheth unto the clouds* [Ps. 108:4].

Further, truth in the Old Testament is what God demands of man. God wants truth within a man, *Behold, thou desirest truth in the inward part* [Ps. 51:6].

And God wants man to speak the truth:

> *LORD, who shall abide* (sojourn) *in thy tabernacle? Who shall dwell in thy holy hill?*
> *He that walketh uprightly, and worketh righteousness, and speaketh the truth in his heart* [Ps. 15:1–2].

God wants man to seek the truth: *if ye can find a man . . . that seeketh the truth* [Jer. 5:1].

He wants man to walk in the truth, *I beseech thee, O Lord, remember now how I have walked before thee in truth and with a perfect heart, and have done that which is good in thy sight* [2 Kgs. 20:3].

And He wants him to conform to His will: *Thou art near, O Lord; and all thy commandments are truth* [Ps. 119:151].

The Old Testament is explicit: God demands of man truth in his whole being, inside him, speaking it, showing it, walking in it, and conforming to it.

Proceeding to the New Testament we find *the truth* stated three ways.

> First, the truth of God is revealed in *Now I say that Jesus Christ was a minister* (became a servant) *of the circumcision for the truth of God, to confirm the promises made unto the fathers* [Rom. 15:8].

> Second, *the truth* of Christ is expressed in [a]*s the truth of Christ is in me* [2 Cor. 11:10].

> Third, the truth of the Gospel as recorded in Paul's Letter to the Galatians, saying, *that the truth of the gospel might continue with you* [Gal. 2:5].

What is revealed in these words? It is all moving to what is called the Christian revelation. It is *the truth* as revealed *in Christ* and *by Christ* and as E. C. Blackman says with emphasis, it takes "precedence over all other human apprehensions of truth." This is seen in the Pastoral letters, most notably in Paul's Second Letter to the Thessalonians where he says,

> *And with all deceivableness* (deception) *of unrighteousness in* (among) *them that perish; because they received not the love of the truth, that they might be saved* [2 Thess. 2:10].
>
> *That they all might be damned who believed not the truth, but had pleasure in unrighteousness* [2 Thess. 2:12].

Paul's words are most important with respect to *the truth* as it is revealed in the Lord Jesus Christ. Please note the importance given to *the truth, the truth* as it is in Jesus. Our Lord Himself prays in His High Priestly prayer, *Sanctify* (set) *them* (apart) *through thy truth: thy word is truth* [John 17:17].

Note it is *the truth* that sanctifies. "Jesus prays that His Father will sanctify them through the truth," as simply, yet forcefully stated by Martyn Lloyd-Jones. Sanctification is not something we achieve by ourselves. If it were, why would Jesus pray for the Father to sanctify us with His truth? The work of sanctification is neither easy nor simple. It is a challenging task, because it means becoming Christlike in our attitude and conduct. Therefore, it requires God working within us as we struggle within ourselves to please Him.

Also, Jesus informs us that the Holy Spirit will guide us to *the truth* after the resurrection. *Howbeit when he, the Spirit of truth, is come, he will guide you into all truth: for he shall not speak of himself* (on his own authority); *but whatsoever he shall hear, that shall he speak: and he will show you things to come* [John 16:13].

Again, we should ask, why is there so much emphasis on *the truth, the truth* as it is in Jesus? Why does Paul exhort us to *put off . . . the old man* and to *put on the new man* [Eph. 4:22, 24]? Why is it that we are not perfect? Why are the church at large and individual congregations as they are?

There are certain thoughts to consider in responding to these questions. First, Paul wants us to know that we continue to exist in our deceitful lusts because we do not have knowledge of *the truth* or do not accept it as we should. We tend to rely on our own mindsets, experiences, or comforts instead of thinking in terms of *the truth* as it is in Jesus.

Second, truth as presented and understood in the context of the New Testament and the Old Testament is to be a stimulant to our actual conduct, not just something to be contemplated. Truth is something we are to do. It is something we either obey or disobey.

> *But he that doeth the truth cometh to the light, that his deeds may be made manifest, that they are wrought in God* [John 3:21].
>
> *If we say that we have fellowship with him, and walk in darkness, we lie, and do not* (practice) *the truth* [1 John 1:6].

The truth fits men for fellowship with God, for fellowship with one another, and for living a good life.

How do we proceed to worshipping God *in spirit and in truth*? Jesus says,

> *Ye worship ye know not what: we know what we worship: for salvation is of the Jews.*
> *But the hour cometh, and now is, when the true worshippers shall worship the Father in spirit and in truth: for the Father seeketh such to worship him.*
> *God is a Spirit: and they that worship him must worship him in spirit and in truth.*
> *The woman saith unto him, I know that Messiah cometh, which is called Christ: when he is come, he will tell us all things.*
> *Jesus saith unto her, I that speak unto thee am he*
> [John 4:22–26].

God requires us to worship Him *in spirit and in truth*. The two go together. The personal embodiment of Jesus as *the truth* can be seen in these verses.

When people come to know *the truth* in Jesus they will worship God in an acceptable manner, and they will live in a way pleasing to the Father. However, such worship and conduct are not possible outside of the Lord Jesus Christ.

The Apostle John expresses this so beautifully,

> *For I rejoiced greatly, when the brethren came and testified of the truth that is in thee, even as thou walkest in the truth.*
> *I have no greater joy than to hear that my children walk in truth*
> [3 John 1:3–4].

How beautiful!

How does the change occur from an existing mindset to being stimulated to exhibit the proper conduct and to worship in *the spirit and the truth*? The change occurs by being renewed in mind and spirit by the grace and power of God. When these things happen we have the

Truth According to God   105

capacity to: seek *the truth*; believe *the truth*; enjoy *the truth*; and grow in grace and in the knowledge of *the truth*.

This happens in regeneration and continues to develop during the sanctification process. All parts of salvation involve a knowledge of *the truth*. Justification is the result of God exercising His will within a person. Our awareness of it involves knowledge. As the Apostle says, *But of him are ye in Christ Jesus, who of God is made unto us* (became for us) *wisdom, and righteousness, and sanctification, and redemption* [1 Cor. 1:30].

The Apostle wants the Ephesians (and us) to know that it is grasping *the truth* that enables us to be righteous and holy. The heart and mind must be involved in obedience and submission. Paul's words to the Romans are most revealing with regard to obedience and submission. They should open our eyes and elicit a positive response. Paul, under the influence of the Holy Spirit, says,

> *Know ye not, that to whom ye yield* (present) *yourselves servants to obey, his servants* (slaves) *ye are to whom ye obey; whether of sin unto death, or of obedience unto righteousness?*
> *But God be thanked, that* (though) *ye were the servants* (slaves) *of sin, but ye have obeyed from the heart that form of doctrine which was delivered you* (to which you were entrusted).
> *Being then made free from sin, ye became the servants of righteousness* [Rom. 6:16–18].

Why did they obey? Because they had seen and believed. They had become capable of so doing. They had been moved to action. The individual is created anew in righteousness and holiness of *the truth*. What is *the truth* that leads to righteousness and holiness?

It is *the truth* about God that brings us to Christ and to God. The only way to ensure that men and women will lead a life that is righteous and holy is for them to know God. This is seen in the Old and New Testaments.

It is found in the teachings of the prophets and in the life of Christ. Jesus brings us to a knowledge of *the truth* and bears witness to it. The Holy Spirit reveals it to us.

The whole purpose of the Gospel is to bring us to a personal knowledge of God. It is not to bring us certain experiences and feelings. It is to bring us into a right relationship with God: it is to know God, to come to a knowledge of *the truth*, and to know *the truth* is the holiness of God. That is the message of the Old Testament and the New Testament. God is truth, God is light.

What else does this truth do? It teaches us about God's utter hatred and abhorrence of sin. It requires understanding the extent to which God hates sin and deceitful lusts. Therefore, we are to *put off the old man* and to *put on the new man* created according to God in righteousness and holiness of *the truth*.

Sanctify (Set) *them* (apart) *through thy truth. Thy word is truth.* What does this redemptive, sanctifying truth reveal? It reveals God's determination to punish sin. He made man in His own image, but man rebelled and disobeyed. Therefore, God drove man out of the Garden of Eden.

God punishes sin. We can read it in the record of the flood, Sodom and Gomorrah, the treatment of the children of Israel, the captivity of Babylon, sending them to Assyria, raising up heathen nations, sending His Son, and crucifying Him on the Cross. This whole record shows God's hatred of sin as well as punishing it. All this is part of God's truth, *the truth as it is in Jesus*. We find this in the Word of God when we study it.

What else are we to do? We are to *put on the new man* created in righteousness and holiness of *the truth*. Who shall have communion with God?

> *Who shall ascend into the hill of the Lord? Or who shall stand in his holy place?*
> *He that hath clean hands, and a pure heart; who hath not lifted up his soul unto vanity* (to an idol), *nor sworn deceitfully.*
> *He shall receive the blessing from the Lord, and righteousness from the God of his salvation.*
> *This is the generation of them that seek him, that seek thy face, O Jacob* [Ps. 24:3–6].

Where does the knowledge of *the truth* lead us? To sanctification. It is through the truth that we are sanctified and come to realize the nature of sin and to hate deceitful lusts.

What is the ultimate purpose of *the truth*, salvation, and sanctification? It is to glorify God and to enjoy Him forever. How do we normally think of this question or answer it? Usually in a self-centered way because the ultimate purpose is our salvation. But that is not the case.

Why has God done for us what he has done? Because He is holy. The objective of salvation and sanctification is to glorify God. Our first objective should be to know Him, to know *the truth* in Christ, and to be well-pleasing in His sight.

Is it any wonder that Paul commands us to *put off . . . the old man* and to *put on the new man, which according to God is created in righteousness and holiness of the truth*?

The question is, how do we *put on the new man*? This question cannot be avoided or evaded. It is addressed to those professing to be followers of Christ, to those saying they have accepted Christ. It is not addressed to those outside Christ. It is something we are to do. But we must realize Christ supplies the power to do it.

Therefore, we are not to shrink from doing it. We are to *put on* the new completely and fully by applying *the truth* to ourselves. This is one of the most important things to discover as members of Christ's body.

How can we apply *the truth* to ourselves? Believe it or not, we are to talk and preach *the truth* to ourselves, but more importantly we are to apply it. When we stumble or fall we are to go back to *the truth* and keep talking, preaching, and practicing it. We are not to be idle or passive, or to wait for something to happen. We are to be active in obeying His commands. As the Apostle Paul says to the Romans, *Likewise reckon* (consider) *ye also yourselves to be dead indeed unto sin, but alive unto God through* (in) *Jesus Christ our Lord* [Rom. 6:11]. Reckon yourself as a new person, as new wineskins for the new wine.

We are to study our Bibles. You have heard this many times in the past. However, say it anew, and accept the fact that there is no better way to learn *the truth* than to become familiar with it. At times we need to be prodded, pricked, or stimulated. Paul wrote to Timothy saying, *Wherefore I put thee in remembrance that thou stir up the gift of God, which is in thee by the putting* (laying) *on of my hands* [2 Tim. 1:6].

The Greek word for *stir* means "rekindle." It conveys the thought that the gift is capable of dying out through neglect if it is not rekindled. The meaning is that the more abundantly God's grace is bestowed upon us the more we should desire to make daily progress in knowing *the truth* as revealed in Christ.

We are to rouse and stimulate ourselves to set the proper priorities. This means learning, reading, and studying under the guidance of the Holy Spirit in order to acquire greater understanding and confidence.

We are to pray that God will enlighten and bless us as we read and study Scripture. We are to pray for wisdom, to give thanks for what He has done within us, and to thank Him for His Son and the Holy Spirit.

We are to have fellowship with fellow saints. We are to assemble together in order to strengthen one another and to support one another. We are to give and receive from one another. The value of our fellowship is with one another. That is why the radio and television ministries will never be a substitute for the church assembled.

The author of the letter to the Hebrews reminds us, *Not forsaking the assembling of ourselves together, . . . but exhorting one another* [Heb. 10:25].

All believers should strive to assemble together, and to bring others into the fellowship. The assembling of the believers is part of the divine pattern. When the saints have fellowship and the Spirit is present, then God acts. "God still works through the Church; the church is His own creation," as Martyn Lloyd-Jones observed.

These three things we are to do: apply *the truth* to ourselves; read and study Scripture; and assemble with other saints. However, there is another reason to consider in putting on the new man. We have no choice. Why do I say that? Because we have been purchased with a price. We are not our own, we are His. We have been bought and purchased with His precious blood. He gave Himself, He climbed the Hill, and He shed His blood.

This is what we are to constantly remember. We are not our own. We belong to Him. We are to remember who we are. Paul tells the Thessalonians, *Ye are all the children* (sons) *of light, and the children* (sons) *of the day: we are not of the night, nor of darkness* [1 Thess. 5:5].

He also tells the Ephesians, *walk as children of the light*. As children of the light, we are to walk as such. Our tenor of life is to exhibit the light. This is to be seen in our demeanor, deportment, attitude, and conduct. We are to become children of light day by day, step by step, piece by piece, and page by page.

How do we do this? Ask the following questions: Where do we start? With *the truth*—Jesus. With whom do we travel? With Jesus—*the truth*. Where do we finish? With *the truth*—Jesus. This is to permeate our minds and hearts.

Paul reminds us that Jesus said, *AND (I) WILL BE A FATHER UNTO YOU, AND YE SHALL BE MY SONS AND DAUGHTERS, saith the Lord Almighty* [2 Cor. 6:18]. As members of the body of Christ we are children of God; therefore, we are to conduct ourselves as His children.

We are to *put on the new man* in truth, and He is to govern our conduct and our activities.

Remember, people are going to judge God, judge the Gospel, and judge Christ by what they see in you and me. It is an awesome thought! It is an awesome responsibility! Of course, people are wrong to judge in that manner, but they do. While we cannot do anything about how they judge us, we can do something about knowing *the truth* and how we are to conduct ourselves.

When we *put on the new man* we should be aware of our responsibilities. Peter says,

> *Dearly beloved, I beseech you as strangers and pilgrims, abstain from fleshly lusts, which war against the soul;*
> *Having your conversation* (conduct) *honest* (honorable) *among the Gentiles: that, whereas they speak against you as evildoers, they may by your good works, which they shall behold, glorify God in the day of visitation* [1 Pet. 2:11–12].

Peter says we are to live, act, and do in order to convince the critics and skeptics, silence them, and affect them in such a manner that they will praise and glorify Him. We must strive not to let Christ down. We are to conduct ourselves as His disciples.

Finally, we are to remember that Christ dwells in our hearts by faith. We are His vessels, His Holy vessels. *Know ye not that ye are the temple of God, and that the Spirit of God dwelleth in you* [1 Cor. 3:16]?

How do we *put on the new man*? By reminding ourselves that Christ dwells within us, by learning *the truth* of God, by learning *the truth* as it is in Jesus, and by conducting ourselves according to God's commands.

What impact will it have? I am reminded of a sermon by Bob Ferguson on the Twenty-third Psalm. At the conclusion he tells about a number of people attending a party, one of whom was a renowned actor. After dinner the conversation turned to religion. One of the guests asked the actor to recite the Twenty-third Psalm. He did. He recited it beautifully, and when he finished there were "ohs" and "ahs" and many compliments.

Also in attendance was an elderly or should we say mature minister. After the congratulatory conversation died down the actor very sincerely asked the minister to say the Twenty-third Psalm and after some encouragement he did so. When he finished saying *And I will dwell in the house of the Lord forever* there was complete silence, there was a hush over the group that lasted a long, long time. Finally, the actor broke the silence saying, "Pastor, I know the Twenty-third Psalm, but you know the Shepherd."

May it be said of us that we know *the truth*, but more importantly that we know the Shepherd, who is *the truth*.

Amen!

13

Speaking the Truth

Wherefore putting away lying, speak every man truth with his neighbor: for we are members one of another [Eph. 4:25].

It occurs frequently when reading Scripture, hearing sermons, or studying the Word that our attention focuses upon a verse or two, or a particular thought that is being expressed. However, we must guard against taking things out of context or overlooking the foundation on which the message is built.

It is important to remember when considering the principles described by Paul that our initial reaction may be to descend from the lofty, eternal purposes of God to more mundane matters such as personal conduct. The focus of our attention may change from heaven to earth, from the heights of eternity to the realities of everyday living, from the sanctity of Christ's life to the darkness of human sin.

Therefore, as we continue walking through Ephesians it is well to remember certain things. The last half of this fourth chapter is referred to by some as a walk in holiness. "This walk involves a radical change in character, what we are in conduct, what we do; in conversation, what we say," as described by Ruth Paxson. The Apostle begins this chapter by beseeching us (calling us to the Lord's side) to *walk worthy of the vocation* (calling) to which we have been called.

He continues by saying,

> *There is one body, and one Spirit . . . one hope; . . . One Lord, one faith, one baptism,*
> *One God and Father of all* [Eph. 4:4–6].

> *For the perfecting* (equipping) *of the saints . . . the edifying of the body of Christ:*
> *Till we all come in* (into) *the unity of the faith, and of the knowledge of the Son of God, unto a perfect* (mature) *man* [Eph. 4:12–13].

Learning the truth as it *is in Jesus* is what Paul tells us to do.

The truths being considered are not just the moral teachings of the Master. Every member of Christ's body potentially possesses every spiritual blessing because he or she is in Christ. However, there are those who profess being in Christ who seem to be poverty-stricken in the spirit, and they seem to have forgotten the incalculable wealth available in Christ. Why?

Perhaps the desire for these treasures may be at low ebb, or the fire within needs to be rekindled, or other desires take precedence over Bible study and worship. Two hours in front of the television may not seem as difficult or long as reading and studying Scripture for thirty minutes.

Putting on the new man means eagerly seeking the riches available in Christ, and setting our affection (mind, thinking) on the things above. Paul reminds the Colossians of their relationship with Christ and where they are to focus their attention when he says, *IF ye then be risen with Christ, seek those things which are above, where Christ sitteth on the right hand of God. Set your affection* (mind) *on things above, not on things on the earth* [Col. 3:1–2].

When seeing what God wants us to do, when having some knowledge and understanding, and when opening our hearts and minds to receive the power of the Holy Spirit, we should seek the things of God and reject the teachings or attractions of men. Paul exhorts us to conform to the teachings of Christ in practical living. By describing godliness and holiness the Apostle wants the followers to eliminate or discard vain human conduct. He wants them to understand the value of being in Christ.

One thing is crystal clear, claiming our position in Christ and coveting our possessions in Him cannot be achieved by relying upon anything that resides within us. It is possible only by and through the power of the Holy Spirit dwelling within. We have received the command to *put off* and to *put on*, but it is the power of the Holy Spirit that works within us to do so. "The Spirit will enable us to walk in righteousness, humility, faith, obedience, lowliness, meekness, forbearance, love, patience, courage, praise and holiness. Our part is to count upon the

Spirit's presence in power to keep self on the Cross and Christ on the throne of our human personality.

"Despite all the difficulties of a walk in a thoroughly defiled and defiling world, God never lowers this standard. However, He is not unreasonable in demanding of us something which we are utterly incapable of doing by ourselves. He (God) has made ample provision for what He requires in giving to us His Holy Spirit and His Holy Word. The Spirit uses the Word in separating us from all that is unholy and in setting us apart to all that is holy. The way of holiness is clearly taught. A daily study of the Word under the tutelage of the Spirit, accompanied by implicit obedience to it, ensures continuous growth into holiness of life.

"The Lord does not discourage us by demanding perfection of character all at once. But our walk should mean a step-by-step growth in Christlikeness; to keep our hearts set on perfection He keeps our eyes fixed on that day—perhaps not far distant—when He will return and the Church will be presented to Him spotless and holy, even as He is," as beautifully stated by Ruth Paxson.

Bearing these things in mind let us turn our attention to *Wherefore, putting away lying, SPEAK EVERY MAN TRUTH WITH HIS NEIGHBOR, for we are members one of another*. Remember, Paul is writing to the members of the body of Christ, the followers in the Way. He is not writing to the secular world, to those outside of Christ. We need to remind ourselves of this constantly.

Paul begins with the word *wherefore*, which means, "on account of" and is an interesting word. It is intended to bring us to grips with spiritual reality and Christ's teachings. The Apostle says "on account of" all the truths previously presented you are to do certain things. You are to take definite action. Paul does not want the Ephesians to be thinking about platitudes. He wants them to put Christ's teachings into action. By using the word *wherefore* he is resolute in wanting to change holy teachings into holy conduct.

"In this word "wherefore" he is insisting that holy character must be transmuted into holy conduct; that it is impossible to have the new man's desires and the old man's deeds; that it is altogether inconsistent to talk of living in the heavenlies while walking in the old haunts of the world. "Wherefore" opens the gate from principle into practice; from the abstract into the concrete; from the general into the particular," as proclaimed by Ruth Paxson.

It is interesting to note how and where the Apostle begins these last few verses of this chapter. First, to emphasize the teachings he uses a contrast everyone can understand: lying—truth. Next, he follows his teaching very logically. He has been stressing the truth as it is in Jesus and proceeds to instruct us about the righteousness and holiness of the truth.

It is important to note how Paul presents this practical teaching. He says, *putting away lying, SPEAK EVERY MAN TRUTH WITH HIS NEIGHBOR: for we are members one of another.* You will note the process: first the negative injunction followed by the positive one, and then the reason for doing both. A good coach or teacher will demonstrate what to do, what not to do, and either state or show how it should be done. Paul uses this method in the next several verses. Why? Because the truth is always to be applied. It is not just to be considered, discussed, or applauded. It is to be put into practice. Knowledge is necessary, but that is not where we are to stop.

If a person truly understands a truth and accepts it, he will put it into practice. This is not easy to do. Paul had a deeper understanding of the human predicament and frailties. He expresses it saying, *The good that I would* (want to do) *I do not: but the evil which I would not, that I do* [Rom. 7:19].

The truth as it is in the Lord Jesus Christ affects the whole of one's life, not just a portion of it. Our conduct reflects how we have learned Christ.

A question to ask as we study this: why does Paul start with lying? Possibly because it provides a sharp contrast to *the truth* contained in the previous verses, or maybe because the Apostle moved logically from *the truth* to lying.

In writing to Titus, Paul stresses the importance of truth that originates with God,

> *PAUL, a servant of God, and an apostle of Jesus Christ, according to the faith of God's elect, and the acknowledging of the truth which is after* (according to) *godliness;*
> *In hope of eternal life, which God, that cannot lie, promised before the world* (time) *began* [Titus 1:1-2].

Note what these verses in Scripture say: *[A]ccording to the faith of God's elect* [Titus 1:1]. Paul says that, "There is a mutual relationship between my Apostleship and the faith of God's elect."

As Calvin puts it, "Therefore, you cannot reject his teaching without being corrupt and a stranger to the true faith in Christ." By the *elect* he means all those from the beginning of the world unto that time and even to this day. Paul refers to the doctrine that agrees with the faith of Abraham and all the other saints. Paul and all his successors make known the same doctrine.

Paul says, *the acknowledging of the truth which is after* (according to) *godliness* [Titus 1:1]. The nature of the Apostle's faith is completely intertwined with knowledge of the truth. Paul points out in his letter to Titus that his message contains only that which is well-known and can instruct people in the pure worship of God.

By using the word *truth*, the Apostle clearly states that faith requires truth. Faith is not to be shaken by probabilities but is to hold fast to what is true. What Paul is holding fast is a particular kind of truth.

> Jesus says, *The Spirit of truth, is come, he will guide you into all truth* [John 16:13].

> Paul says, . . . *who hath bewitched you, that ye should not obey the truth*, . . . [Gal. 3:1].

> Colossians says, *Whereof ye heard before in the word of the truth of the gospel* [Col. 1:5].

> *The church of the living God, the pillar and ground* (standing) *of the truth* [1 Tim. 3:15].

In this instance, the church is the called-out, not a building, which is what we commonly think of when referring to the church. The pillar is a pillar, but the ground means to lay a foundation.

Therefore, this verse should read, "The called out of the living God, the foundation and pillar of the truth." Paul says this is *How thou oughtest to behave thyself in the house of the living God's truth*. As we can readily see, the truth is a pure and right knowledge of God, and Jesus Christ is that Truth providing knowledge of God. This knowledge is provided to free us from falsehood.

It is truth, *[W]hich is after* (according to) *godliness* [Titus 1:1]. This phrase qualifies the truth of which Paul has been speaking. It is directed toward the right worship of God and to preserving His teachings among men.

[W]hich God, that cannot lie [Titus 1:2] is added not only to glorify God, but to reaffirm our faith. When God's teachings and our relationship to Him are considered we should remember that it is founded "on the Word of Him who cannot deceive or lie," according to John Calvin's appropriate description. These teachings should help us to better understand what the Apostle is saying.

Paul is not just saying that lying is a terrible thing and therefore we should not do it. He is not stating a moralist or humanist point of view. He is saying we are to put away lying because we are reconciled to God, have fellowship with Him, and are members of Christ's body.

We are to put away lying because we know Him, and we are to keep His commandments. *He that saith, I know him, and keepeth not his commandments, is a liar, and the truth is not in him* [1 John 2:4]. As Lloyd-Jones says, "To know God and to have fellowship with God means of necessity, truth and truthfulness." God demands honesty and truthfulness in the inner man.

When realizing this, we begin to see why the Apostle, led by the Holy Spirit, begins this portion of Scripture by saying, *Wherefore putting away lying, speak every man truth with his neighbor* [Eph. 4:25]. God represents truth, whereas the devil represents the opposite—lying.

> *Why do ye not understand my speech? even because ye cannot hear my word.*
> *Ye are of your father the devil, and the lusts* (desires) *of your father ye will do. He was a murderer from the beginning, and abode* (stands) *not in the truth, because there is no truth in him. When he speaketh a lie, he speaketh of his own* (from his own nature): *for he is a liar, and the father of it* [John 8:43–44].

Note how brusquely and forthrightly Jesus deals with truth and lying. As members of the body of Christ, we are required to see the evil in lying and to know where it originates.

Man is separated from God because, *The serpent beguiled Eve through his subtilty* [2 Cor. 11:3]. The occasion of the first sin was a lie. There are certain unique characteristics about a lie or lying. First, it is probably the most prevalent and common trait in the life of sin. It is evident in everyday living, in the practical aspects of life. A person commits an evil act, whether it be a so-called major or minor one, and what happens? They do not want anyone to find out, so they tell a lie, and then developments occur resulting in more lies being told. This is characteristic of the life apart from Christ. It happens in all phases of society and in every type of culture. Unfortunately, society and social functions are plagued by lies and conditions having their basis in lying. They exhibit pretence, sham, and play-acting, all of which have their roots in the lie.

Second, the lie is one of the main contributors to the complications encountered in living. Why do things become so complicated, involved, and difficult? Normally because there is a lack of truth or because falsehoods have been stated or inferred. The classic example is when a person tells a so-called trivial story to cover up a wrong and then has to tell another, and another, and another. As a result of the original lie, life becomes more complicated and involved. And the process goes on and on and on.

When thinking about it, is there anything that causes as much misery and unhappiness in the world as lying and all of its subtleties, shams, and deceits? Just try to think of the havoc that is caused by lies, of the suffering inflicted upon innocent people, all because of the innumerable categories of lies.

When considering all the ramifications of lying, is there any wonder that the Apostle deals with this item first? When pursuing this matter it is only natural that sooner or later we must ask, what is the essence of lying, what causes it? The answer is rather evident, if we are willing to objectively consider it. It is self: self-centeredness, selfishness, self-regard, self-importance, and self-rationalization.

What does this have to do with lying? We express ourselves through speech, and when we do we are subject to temptations of various types: praise, importance, and accomplishments. Consequently, we engage in misstatements, exaggerations, embellishments, coloring the details, fabrications, half-truths, inventions, withholdings, and rationalizations. Each of these contributes to the various aspects of lying.

Third, there is one universal or all-encompassing characteristic of lying. If you would ask people of all walks of life, cultures, nationalities, countries, and ages what they think of a person who is a liar, you would get the same answer from all the different categories.

They would probably state that it is the most common and most universal of all sins. Some people commit certain sins, while others commit different ones. But lying is common to all, in one or more of its various forms. Though most everyone despises and denounces a lie, it is something everyone is guilty of in one form or another. It is something that originates within the depths of a person. It reveals the depth of sin and the power it exercises. The irony of it is that though we despise it, we do it.

Fourth, there is nothing more hostile to the believers of the Old and New Testaments than lying. Paul writes to the Colossians, *Lie not one to another, seeing that ye have put off the old man with his deeds* [Col. 3:9].

As we have seen, Paul measures a person's living against the truth in Jesus, or the true word of the Gospel. Falsehood exhibits disloyalty to Christ.

Here we have the command: SPEAK EVERYMAN TRUTH WITH HIS NEIGHBOR. What does this include? The express responsibility is to be witnesses to the revelation. The command is to follow Christ, to show unselfish love, and to build up our fellow members in Christ.

The Old Testament concept of truth was translated by the word *faithfulness*. This underlies the meaning of SPEAK EVERYMAN TRUTH where it is translated "to talk, tell, and speak the truth."

In writing to the Ephesians, Paul directs his comments to the called-out. He is not writing to those who are not members of the body of Christ. He is dealing with the whole aspect of living as members one with another. Therefore, if we lie to one another, we are in a sense lying to ourselves and to the Head of the body. We do not live independently or exist separately. The Spirit dwells among the assembled believers.

The hand or foot is not separate from the body. If a finger or toe is burned or has a thorn in it the whole body suffers. The members of Christ's body bear testimony and witness to one another according to the unity and peace created by the Lord Jesus Christ.

In closing, another question: how can there be true fellowship if there is lying instead of speaking the truth? True fellowship is marked by mutual trust, dependence, and confidence, enabling one to speak openly and freely. When lying enters into the fellowship, then the elements that created it are destroyed, whether it be family, class, congregation, or the mafia. Lying makes unity impossible.

Jesus said in response to the question,

> . . . *which is the great commandment in the law?*
> . . . THOU SHALT LOVE THE LORD THY GOD WITH ALL THY HEART AND WITH ALL THY SOUL, AND WITH ALL THY MIND [Matt. 22:36–37].

> *. . . And the second* (commandment) *is like unto it, THOU SHALT LOVE THY NEIGHBOR AS THYSELF* [Matt. 22:39].

As we well know, it is detrimental to try to fool or to lie to ourselves. The same is true with God, our neighbor, and other members of Christ's body.

We are to be children of light, not of darkness. We are to *put off* the old and to *put on* the new. It is difficult, if not impossible, to lie if our attention and affection are focused on the Lord Jesus Christ.

If we are truly members of His body, then lying is to be *put off*. Remember, we are children of God, the God who cannot lie, the God who is truth. Jesus said, *I am the way, the truth, and the life: No man cometh unto the Father, but by me* [John 14:6].

> The Apostle Paul, following in his Master's footsteps, says, *Wherefore putting away lying, SPEAK EVERY MAN TRUTH WITH HIS NEIGHBOR: for we are members one of another* [Eph. 4:25].

May we be obedient to His command by *putting away lying*.
Amen!

14

Anger—Sinful or Righteous

> *Be ye angry, and sin not: let not the sun go down upon your wrath* [Eph. 4:26].

Previously, we focused attention upon lying and the truth. Now we consider another of the Apostle's prohibitions, commandments, and motivations. The negative injunction is *Be ye angry, and sin not*. The positive injunction is . . . *let not the sun go down upon your wrath*. And the logical reason is *Neither give place* (an opportunity) *to the devil* [Eph. 4:27].

There is a word of precaution to keep in the forefront of our minds as we hear God's word. We are to focus on the Lord Jesus Christ, not on ourselves. He has specific reasons for revealing His teachings, for illuminating Paul's heart and mind, and for preserving these words of instruction. Therefore, remember the mindset. We are to put our own experiences and thinking in the background. Paul is writing to mature adults as far as years go. Also, he is writing to members of Christ's body, who are growing in their faith and developing their characters, conduct, and commitment.

The Apostle penned this letter after his conversion on the road to Damascus. Therefore, you can be sure he had thoughts from his previous life about anger, wrath, sin, and the devil.

Anger is a common sin among people of all ages. For the most part, we would just as soon never experience it, express it, or be exposed to it ever again. It appears in various ways: smoldering resentment, sudden outbursts, sullenness, intimidating acts and words, violent expressions, malice, and vendettas. Then there are the results: remorse, regret, indulgence, hardness, and either real forgiveness or the complete lack of it.

Anger—Sinful or Righteous

Anger comes in many different packages, and for the most part it never comes at the right time.

Is it not interesting that immediately after the Apostle exhorts the followers to *put off* the old, and to *put on* the new, he presents common maladies that can have a negative impact upon the three C's: character, conduct, and conversation (tenor of life)?

Probably one reason for doing this is because sin breaks fellowship. Two things definitely affecting fellowship are lying and anger. What promotes fellowship? Holiness and following in the footsteps of the Lord Jesus. Therefore, Paul addresses those things having a negative impact upon fellowship among the members of Christ's body. Then he provides a positive command and the reason for so doing.

There are people who believe and suggest that anger should be eliminated or suppressed in all its various forms. However, that is not the teaching of Scripture. As R. W. Dale said, "Anger in itself is not sinful." We are all aware of the fact that at times Christ was angry. What is wrong with being angry at unlawful acts of aggression, hypocrisy, cruelty, and other evil acts? It is not wrong to be angry at those things.

However, our anger is to be governed, controlled, and expressed in the right manner according to the teachings of our Master. It is not to be exhibited by violence, maliciousness, degenerate revenge, or succumbing to evil temptations.

When do we sin in anger? When the root cause of the anger is self and the anger is directed against the sinner instead of the sin. When our feelings are hurt and self gets in the way. When we are not angry for the glory of Jesus Christ. Note, Paul did not respond in anger when he was treated badly in presenting the Gospel.

What faults offend God when we are angry? According to Calvin there are three: "The first is when we are angry from slight causes, and often from none, or private injuries or offenses. The second is when we go too far, and are carried into intemperate excesses. The third is when our anger, which ought to have been directed against ourselves or against sins, is turned against our brethren. Most appropriately, . . . Paul, when he wished to describe the limitation of anger, employs the well known passage, *Be ye angry, and sin not*.

"This we do, if we seek the object of our anger in ourselves rather than in others, if we pour out our indignation against our own faults. As to others, we ought to be angry at their faults rather than at their persons, nor ought we to be excited to anger by private offences; but zeal for the glory of God should inflame our anger. Lastly, our anger ought to be allowed to subside, lest it should mix itself with the violent affections of the flesh."

What else does the Apostle mean by this phrase, *be angry and sin not*? We are to seek the object of our anger in ourselves rather than in others. However, we are prone to say, "He did this to me" or "She did that to me." So we become angry at the person. We are to look past the person to the cause of the transgression. We are to look at our own sinful natures and our lack of obedience to the will of God and His commandments. Our anger should be directed to the faults or sins, not to the person. Certainly, we should not become angry at personal offences. This is difficult, but it is to be practiced.

Basically, the only thing that should inflame our anger is zeal for the glory of God. However, it is to be controlled and governed by the Lord Jesus Christ. Certainly, we are not to become zealots.

God's anger or wrath toward sin is not an irrational, impulsive, irresponsible action or expression. When the sins of God's people bring forth His anger or wrath it is accompanied by His forbearance and mercy. *O Lord, I have heard thy speech, and was afraid: O Lord, revive thy work in the midst of the years, in the midst of the years make known; in wrath remember mercy* [Hab. 3:2]. What did our Lord Jesus Christ say?

> *AND he entered again into the synagogue; and there was a man there which had a withered hand.*
>
> *And they watched him, whether he would heal him on the sabbath day; that they might accuse him.*
>
> *And he saith unto the man which had the withered hand, Stand forth* (arise from the middle).
>
> *And he saith unto them, Is it lawful to do good on the sabbath days, or to do evil? to save life, or to kill? But they held their peace* (kept silent).
>
> *And when he had looked round about on them with anger, being grieved for the hardness of their hearts, he saith unto the man, Stretch forth thine hand. And he stretched it out: and his hand was restored whole as the other* [Mark 3:1–5].

> *After this he went down to Capernaum, he, and his mother, and his brethren, and his disciples: and they continued there not many days.*
>
> *And the Jews' passover was at hand, and Jesus went up to Jerusalem,*

> *And found in the temple those that sold oxen and sheep and doves, and the changers of money sitting:*
>
> *And when he had made a scourge (whip) of small cords, he drove them all out of the temple, and the sheep, and the oxen; and poured out the changers' money, and overthrew (overturned) the tables;*
>
> *And said unto them that sold doves, Take these things hence; make not my Father's house a house of merchandise.*
>
> *And his disciples remembered that it was written, THE ZEAL OF THINE HOUSE HATH EATEN ME UP* [John 2:12–17].

Note the words and actions of our Lord, His anger at the hardness of their hearts, cleansing the temple, driving out the moneychangers and traders.

Paul wrote to the Romans and said,

> *For I am not ashamed of the gospel of Christ: for it is the power of God unto salvation to every one that believeth; to the Jew first, and also to the Greek* [Rom. 1:16]
>
> *. . . For the wrath of God is revealed from heaven against all ungodliness and unrighteousness of men, who hold* (suppress) *the truth in unrighteousness* [Rom. 1:18].

Note that Paul said, *For I am not ashamed of the gospel of Christ . . . For the wrath of God is revealed from heaven against all ungodliness and unrighteousness of men.*

The Apostle expresses it in more detail in 2 Corinthians,

> *For though I made you sorry with a letter, I do not repent* (regret it), *though I did repent* (regret it): *for I perceive that the same epistle hath made you sorry, though it were but for a season* (while).
>
> *Now I rejoice, not that ye were made sorry, but that ye sorrowed to repentance: for ye were made sorry after* (according to) *a godly manner, that ye might receive damage by* (suffer loss from) *us in nothing.*
>
> *For godly sorrow worketh repentance to salvation not to be repented* (regretted) *of: but the sorrow of the world worketh death.*
>
> *For behold this selfsame thing, that ye sorrowed after a godly sort* (manner), *what carefulness* (diligence) *it wrought in you, yea, what clearing of yourselves, yea, what indignation, yea, what fear, yea, what vehement desire, yea, what zeal, yea, what revenge* (vindication)*! In all things ye have approved* (proved) *yourselves to be clear in this matter* [2 Cor. 7:8–11].

Paul rebuked the Corinthians in his earlier letter. Then he received positive reports about the Corinthians, so he toned down his comments. However, it should be noted that Paul was not displeased with what he had written earlier nor was he retracting any part of it. He had written under the guidance of the Holy Spirit. He was pleased by their response.

Paul did not delight in their sorrow. He was trying to promote their welfare and their happiness. Consequently, he employed harsh remedies. He did this because the Corinthians were important to him and he loved them.

Paul contrasts godly sorrow with the sorrow of the world as he says, *For godly sorrow worketh repentance to salvation not to be repented* (regretted) *of: but the sorrow of the world worketh death* [2 Cor. 7:10].

There is also a contrast between godly joy and worldly joy. In godly joy people look to God for their happiness, and they receive pleasure from His grace by being obedient to His commandments and having fellowship with Him.

Godly sorrow is when people look up to God and are in misery because they are separated from His grace. This type of sorrow is the first step in repentance. This is important and should be considered carefully. If a sinner is not dissatisfied with himself and angry with his sin, then he will not accept the Lord Jesus Christ.

When a person experiences godly sorrow, he will have a change of heart. He will *put off* the old and *put on* the new. A person cannot do this until there is a hatred of sin and remorse over disobeying God's commands, followed by repentance. When this happens, repentance is accompanied by joy and thanksgiving for a new, meaningful relationship with the Lord Jesus Christ, God the Father, and the Holy Spirit. Why? Because it brings forth precious fruit whose seed will multiply.

What does the Apostle mean when he says, *Yea, what indignation*? When there is godly sorrow the person is angry with his own faults and himself. Why is this so? Because he or she realizes that the offense, whatever it may have been, has been committed against God.

Two things should be quite apparent. First, evil thoughts or actions should displease us. Second, they should rouse us to controlled, justifiable anger so that we will deal with ourselves forthrightly and severely. We should punish sins wherever we find them, beginning with ourselves. If we do not realize these various actions offend God, then we will not be moved to righteous living, and we will not deal with them as we should. The psalmist says,

> *Ye that love the Lord, hate evil: he preserveth the souls of his saints; he delivereth them out of the hand of the wicked.*
> *Light is sown for the righteous, and gladness for the upright in heart.*
> *Rejoice in the Lord, ye righteous; and give thanks at the remembrance (for the memory) of his holiness* (his holy name)
> [Ps. 97:10–12].

We must learn to love and rejoice in God's righteousness. By the same token we are to learn to hate evil, sin, and iniquity.

When a sense of shame, anger, or righteous indignation against sin is absent, it is usually accompanied by degradation, sinfulness, and disobedience to God, or there may not be a relationship with Him. Though we may exhibit anger, we are not to sin.

Following his negative injunction, the Apostle provides us with a positive commandment: *Let not the sun go down upon your wrath*. Please note that the Apostle does not use the word anger in this phrase. He uses the Greek word *parorgismos*, which means, "provoking to anger." Therefore, this phrase should read, "Let not the sun go down upon you while you are provoking to anger or provoking yourself to anger."

Under the influence of the Holy Spirit, Paul realizes that a person at times may give way to wrong or sinful anger. However, he exhorts us not to let it smolder or simmer. We are not to add fuel to the fire. As members of Christ's body, we are to suppress and rid ourselves of the anger, and not allow it to harden within our hearts and minds. This is difficult, but that is what we are to do!

The word *wrath* in this phrase has a further connotation. It means anger that is nourished and nurtured until it becomes a person's way of life. The individual becomes controlled by worldly sorrows: he or she becomes bitter, vindictive, and determined to seek vengeance.

That is the type of wrath that the Apostle means. However, as we have seen, that is not God's wrath. The Apostle in this phrase is condemning the wrong type of anger. As we have seen, anger is never to be personal. It should always be against the principle of iniquity and sin.

Therefore, if we become angry during the day or evening hours, we are to take steps before we close our eyes to overcome the anger and to have a right relationship with God. It is difficult to draw nigh unto God when we are controlled by an emotion like sinful anger.

When we are controlled by emotion it is difficult to think rationally, to reason, and to consider developments in an objective manner. Therefore, the Apostle says, *Neither give place* (an opportunity) *to the devil* [Eph. 4:27].

Paul knows full well that a person filled with anger or wrath is subject to *the wiles* (schemes) *of the devil* and to doing things that he or she will regret. The word *devil* means "the one who is instigating a man to sin," which is similar to the meaning in the third chapter of Genesis. It means to tempt a person to do evil and encouraging him or her to do so by deception.

Sinful anger leads to nursing grievances, desiring revenge, despising people, and treating them contemptibly. When sinful anger takes over, watch out! For it is then that the devil pounces, causing pain and discomfort.

What is the Apostle teaching about sinful anger and the bitter fruit it produces? To become vindictive, vengeful, or hardened as a result of anger is to deny the basic teachings of our Master. We are members of His body solely by the grace of God. How can we have this type disposition? How can we say the Lord's Prayer if we are contemplating the acts of sinful anger? What is the contrast to sinful anger? What does our Lord say about forgiveness and forgiving others?

Peter asked the Lord Jesus if he should forgive his brother who sinned against him seven times. Jesus answered, saying, *I say not unto thee, Until seven times: but, Until seventy times seven* [Matt. 18:22].

Then he tells the parable of the servant who owed his master ten thousand talents, an astronomical amount. The largest number in the Greek language was ten thousand. One talent was a seventy-five pound gold piece which was the largest unit of money. The value of the ten thousand talents was beyond comprehension. What did the servant who owed this amount to his master do? He begged for patience and compassion and his master forgave him the debt. What did he do then? He immediately found the man who owed him only one hundred pence, a pittance, grabbed him by the throat, and demanded payment. Further, he showed neither patience nor compassion, and cast the person into prison. Jesus closes this parable by saying, *So likewise shall my heavenly Father do also unto you, if ye from your hearts forgive not every one his brother their trespasses* [Matt. 18:35].

If you cannot forgive your brother or sister who truly asks for forgiveness, then you are not forgiven yourself. We are to *put off* the old and *put on* the new. If I claim that I have accepted the Lord Jesus Christ, if I claim to be a member of His body, then I must do unto others what God has done for me. If I do that, then I cannot be angry in a sinful manner, I will not give place to the devil, and the sun will not set on my wrath. Remember, Scripture says,

> *Dearly beloved, avenge not yourselves, but rather give place unto wrath: for it is written, VENGEANCE IS MINE; I WILL REPAY, SAITH THE LORD.*
> *Therefore IF THINE ENEMY HUNGER, FEED HIM; IF HE THIRST, GIVE HIM DRINK: FOR IN SO DOING THOU SHALT HEAP COALS OF FIRE ON HIS HEAD.*
> *Be not overcome of evil, but overcome evil with good*
> [Rom. 12:19–21].

Pray God that the teachings of Scripture will give us new insights into these verses: *BE YE ANGRY AND SIN NOT: let not the sun go down upon your wrath. Neither give place* (an opportunity) *to the devil* [Eph. 4:26–27].

We can be angry at those things that anger God and the Lord Jesus Christ. However, we are not to yield to sinful anger. Further, we are not to let the sun set on our anger. We are to yield to God and be obedient unto Him.

We are to hate the sin but never the sinner. Lastly, we are to address the sin within ourselves. We are to hate it, we are to deal with it, and we are to turn to God in repentance. Sin must always be condemned. It is never to be condoned.

Some people do not like to hear that. They will ask, what about mercy, grace, compassion, and love? These principles and characteristics of God are to be directed toward the repentant sinner.

However, the sinner should have a holy anger toward the sin, he should want to do away with it, whenever, wherever, and however it occurs. He should not defend himself for committing the sin nor rationalize about it. Scripture is rather explicit and presents a very balanced picture: hatred of sin, not hatred of the sinner.

Anger? Yes, but according to the teachings of Christ. The Apostle exhorts us, *Let not the sun go down upon your wrath.* We are not to allow anger to blind us and to keep us from seeing the truth as it is in Jesus.

This may mean that we will have to struggle and wrestle with something before we finally go to sleep. It means that we have to include the Lord Jesus Christ in our reasoning and in our discussions. It means we have to see the love of God in Christ within us as members of the body of Christ. It means we see Christ on the Cross so that our sins might be forgiven. It means that we are grateful and thankful for His mercy and forbearance.

He forgives us of the sins we commit against ourselves and others: can we do less?

We are to cleanse ourselves of sinful anger. Why? Primarily for the glory of God and the love of Christ. Secondly, so that we might live in a right relationship with God and with each other. If we do *not* do this, then we will make a place for the devil, who will take possession of our hearts when we allow anger or wrath to endure.

As our Lord said in the Sermon on the Mount,

> *No man can serve two masters: for either he will hate the one, and love the other; or else he will hold* (be loyal) *to the one, and despise the other. Ye cannot serve God and mammon* (riches)
> [Matt. 6:24].

We are to examine and apply the teachings of Jesus from His perspective, not ours. Therefore, we are to acquire knowledge and understanding from Him and apply it.

> *BE YE ANGRY AND SIN NOT; let not the sun go down upon your wrath:*
> *Neither give place* (an opportunity) *to the devil*
> [Eph. 4:26–27].

These are challenging words, comforting words, demanding words. However, first and foremost they are God's words, and we are to obey them.

Amen!

15

Steal No More, Labor, and Give to the Needy

> *Let him that stole steal no more: but rather let him labor, working with his hands the thing which is good, that he may have to give to him that needeth* [Eph. 4:28].

The third injunction presented by the Apostle after exhorting the hearers to *put off* the old and to *put on* the new is a common one and something about which everyone has definite ideas. It has many variations, appears almost everywhere, and is very difficult to handle, especially according to the Master's teachings. Therefore, it is important to open our minds, to not only hear but to understand what Scripture says, *Let him that stole steal no more: but rather let him labor, . . . that he may have to give to him that needeth.*

In this verse there is the prohibition—steal no more; commandment—labor; and the motivation—to give to the needy. Is that not interesting? The reason for laboring is to give to the needy, not for self-satisfaction, accumulating wealth, or satisfying one's desires. There is not another reason given for laboring—only giving to the needy. They are to be the beneficiaries of the saint's labor.

Note that Scripture says, *let him labor, . . . that he may have to give to him that needeth*. This is a command, not a request. It does not say to give out of your abundance, or to whom you are to give. However, it does say you are to labor, and you are to give a portion of what you earn, whether it be very little or very much, to the needy.

When considering this Scripture it is well to remember other truths. Recall the verse, *And that ye put on the new man, which after God is created in righteousness and true holiness* [Eph. 4:24]. This is followed by the Apostle directing attention to three human characteristics known to all people: lying, anger, and stealing.

What does Scripture say about the person who steals, the thief?

> *Know ye not that the unrighteous shall not inherit the kingdom of God? Be not deceived: neither fornicators* (the sexually immoral), *nor idolators, nor adulterers, nor effeminate* (homosexuals), *nor abusers of themselves* (sodomites) *with mankind,*
> *Nor thieves, nor covetous, nor drunkards, nor revilers, nor extortioners, shall inherit the kingdom of God* [1 Cor. 6:9–10].

The Apostle says that the person who persists in stealing is not a member of the body of Christ, or a Christian, in the modern vernacular.

Each point the Apostle presents during the last seven verses of this fourth chapter and in the first two verses of the fifth chapter is important and should not be overlooked. Each one is to be applied and to become part of our daily living and practice. We are called to exhibit Christlike conduct, therefore, we are to know, understand, accept and practice what Scripture says, if we are in Christ and walking as one of His disciples.

Why? For the glory of God, first and foremost. Next, because of our relationship to other people, and lastly, for ourselves. We are not to overlook any of these injunctions, nor are we to give them short shrift.

What are the negative injunctions?

> *Putting away lying;*
> *BE YE ANGRY AND SIN NOT;*
> *Steal no more;*
> *Let no corrupt communication proceed out of your mouth;*
> *Grieve not the holy Spirit of God;*
> *Let all bitterness, and wrath, and anger, andclamor, and evil speaking, be put away* [Selections from Eph. 4:25–31].

Whereas the positive injunctions are:

> *SPEAK EVERY MAN TRUTH WITH HIS NEIGHBOR;*
> *Let not the sun go down upon your wrath;*
> *Let him labor, working with his hands;*
> *(Speak) that which is good to the use of edifying;*
> *Be ye kind to one another, tenderhearted;*
> *Forgiving one another;*
> *BE ye . . . followers of God; and*
> *Walk in love* [Selections from Eph. 4:25–5:2].

What are the reasons or motivations for eliminating the negative and putting on the positive?

> *For we are members one of another;*
> *Neither give place* (an opportunity) *to the devil;*
> *Give to him that needeth:*
> *Minister grace unto the hearers;*
> *God, for Christ's sake hath forgiven* (in Christ forgave) *you; and*
> *Christ . . . hath given himself for us an offering and a sacrifice to*
> *God for a sweet-smelling savor* (aroma)
> [Selections from Eph. 4:25–5:2].

Hopefully, placing these items in categories provides a better perspective of the teachings and applying them.

How is the Gospel to be applied to these teachings? First, the Gospel of Jesus Christ is for sinners, and that includes all of us. The negative and positive injunctions are tailored to the followers as well as the reasons and motivations.

Though it is difficult, and some say impossible, to abide by these injunctions, there is a way. What is it? The power of the Gospel. Why? Because there is nothing beyond the power of the Gospel.

When addressing each item, we need to realize and believe that when the power of the Gospel enters into a person's life it is of such magnitude that it allows someone to overcome the negative and *put on* the positive. Each person can loose the bonds that hold him or her captive and set them free.

Second, the Gospel keeps us from different types of sins and the varying degrees of each one. The capability to do so depends upon our condition and relationship to Jesus Christ, plus our knowledge, understanding, and mindset.

There is a question to consider: why does the Apostle speak directly about lying, anger, and stealing, especially at this point in his letter? People often say they thought Paul was writing to new creatures in Christ, to those who had recently *put off* the old and *put on* the new, to those who had been regenerated. Therefore, why stress these unacceptable practices and transgressions of God's commandments? Unfortunately, people look at the surface and do not examine what is beneath it. We are to realize there is more to these injunctions than initially apparent. People remind us that Scripture says, *Therefore, any man be in Christ, he is a new creature* (creation): *old things are passed away; behold, all things are become new* [2 Cor. 5:17].

These words are often misinterpreted. Some say that what was true of a person before he believed, before he accepted Christ, have disappeared, have gone away. Further, that nothing remains of the old self in that person's character or conduct. Obviously, that is not true. It is not an accurate interpretation of Scripture. If that interpretation were true then Paul never would have written to the Ephesians. He would not have had to tell them: *Wherefore, putting away lying; . . . Be ye angry, and sin not; . . . steal no more.*

Those outside Christ misinterpret Scripture; they misunderstand what happens to the person who becomes a member of Christ's body. The person outside Christ thinks those in Christ ought to be perfect. He does not realize that we are not perfect, that we do not claim to be perfect, and that we need the power of the Gospel to strengthen us and to keep us from sin.

A person who becomes a new creature may be delivered from particular sins without any real effort. He or she may not need additional power or instruction through all the days allocated to each one, but he or she needs the power of the Holy Spirit to strengthen and sustain him or her.

One thing is certain, being a new creature in Christ does not automatically deliver us from all our sins. Nor does it make us immune from every conceivable temptation.

The New Testament reveals that first we become babes in Christ. We do not become adults at once, or overnight. We are babes, and we need to grow. To mature we need instruction, learning, growing in grace, knowledge of the Lord Jesus Christ, and the power of the Holy Spirit.

When this happens it is important to recognize that although we may see the broad picture, the landscape, the buildings, and the library, it is equally important to know the individual components as well as the strength and beauty of each one. Therefore, the Apostle wants us to examine each individual part, to study it, and to apply it.

Lying, anger, and stealing are common sins to all lands and peoples. They are often condoned. Therefore, the Apostle addresses things that are known to all people. He says, *Let him that stole steal no more.*

What does this mean? Stealing does not just mean items or material things. It means taking possession of and using anything that does not belong to you. It means serving your own ends and gratifying your desires. It applies to things other than money. It can apply to time, to ideas, to articles, and to possessions belonging to another which you regard as your own.

The Apostle says, *Let him that stole steal no more.* Possibly nothing is more degrading than stealing. It involves stealth, concealment, furtiveness, misusing one's abilities, and coveting what belongs to another. It means misusing what talents and capabilities God has given you. It involves misusing brain power, reasoning ability, logic, planning, and ingenuity. Unfortunately, the stealer receives a perverted sense of pleasure from it.

Why does a person steal? What is behind it? Basically, it is selfishness—the desire to have, to possess something, and to get what one wants. It is the desire to have without exerting honest effort. Apparently, the thief dislikes working legitimately.

The person who fails to see the dignity of work and the rightness of it soon begins to think in terms of having instead of earning. When that happens, the door opens to some form of dishonesty. The mere having, getting, or enjoying is not the ultimate. It is accompanied by a dislike or distaste for honest labor and effort.

The maxim of getting without giving certainly is not irreligious. However, the person who steals persuades himself that he has a right to whatever he may desire or want. He does not ask to whom it belongs, he merely wants it and takes it. When people do this, they are putting self first and showing a lack of respect for things that belong to other people. It gets back to childish thinking and action. I want what I want—it's mine because I want it.

The result of taking what belongs to others is that it makes fellowship impossible. I imagine that if thieves began to steal from each other, their fellowship would soon end.

There cannot be unity and fellowship where each one takes what he wants even though it belongs to another. In this respect, the Apostle is concerned with the lesser offenses as well as the ones punishable by law. The ones that are concealed and subtle, as well as the ones that are open and blatant. Why? Because any such action is against the will of God. It expresses selfishness and placing oneself in a priority position.

What does Scripture say we are to do? . . . *but rather let him labor, working with his hands the thing which is good.* Note, Paul does not just say stop doing those things or abstain from doing them, he says do something positive. He prescribes a positive rule. We are to supply our desires and needs by labor, not at the expense of others or by taking from them.

He does not say pray about it, or let go and let God, or the situation will take care of itself, or sit back and analyze everything before you do anything. No, he immediately says to labor. The word for *labor* he uses is the Greek word *kopiao*. It means "to grow weary by toiling." "It means working to the point of fatigue," is the way Martyn Lloyd-Jones states it.

It is the same word the Apostle uses in:

> *Yea, ye yourselves know, that these hands have ministered unto* (provided for) *my necessities, and to them that were with me.*
> *I have showed you all things, how that so labouring ye ought to support the weak, and to remember the words of the Lord Jesus, how he said, It is more blessed to give than to receive* [Acts 20:34–35].

> *And labor, working with our own hands: being reviled, we bless; being persecuted, we suffer* (endure) *it:*
> *Being defamed* (slandered), *we entreat* (encourage): *we are made as the filth of the world, and are the offscouring of all things unto this day* [1 Cor. 4:12–13].

The New Testament stresses and upholds the dignity of work. As people stray from God, they do not listen to Him or obey His commandments but become lazier and less dependent upon their own labor. A person can grow weary and tired from his or her own labor only when he or she really exerts themselves. This is true whether it be real physical labor or exercising the little gray cells adroitly, dexterously, and diligently.

It is to enjoy working, to enjoy creating something, and to see the fruit of one's labor. When people do this, they are usually able to provide for themselves and have something left over to supply to the needs of others.

Paul emphasized work in his letters. Most rabbis of Paul's time worked at some trade or profession. Labor is neither a curse nor a punishment. It is an integral part of God's plan. Our primary objective is not leisure and pleasure. No, we are to labor, we are to enjoy it, and we are to grow weary from our toils.

It is interesting and revealing to note the difference between the attitude of the Greek and the Hebrew.

The Greeks considered work as something to be left to slaves or mechanics. "Aristotle's perfect man will not soil his hands with it," according to Alan Richardson.

On the other hand the Hebrews regarded it as a divine command. *Six days shalt thou labor, and do all thy work* [Exod. 20:9]. Throughout Scripture labor is treated as a divine ordinance of life.

Paul exhorts us to work, to labor. No one is to steal or to take from another. Even if a person pleads that they are in want, they are to labor.

Then Paul provides the motivating reason for not stealing and for laboring, *that he may have to give to him that needeth*. Again Paul turns the person's attention from focusing inwardly to focusing on others. He does not say labor so that you can accumulate or have abundant resources, but that you may have *to give to him that needeth*. What a difference from today's world.

An individual's labor is not for personal gratification only. It is to glorify God, to be a good steward, and to give to those *that needeth*. Scripture says *to give to him that needeth*. It is an all encompassing statement. It does not say to the poor or any particular group. It covers all worthy individuals, groups, or organizations that "may have a need of something," or "to supply that which (is) needed in each case," or "as the need may be," as defined in Vines Expository Dictionary of New Testament Words.

As God's stewards, we are to be faithful. *Let a man so account of* (consider) *us, as of the ministers* (servants) *of Christ, and stewards of the mysteries of God. Moreover it is required in stewards, that a man be found faithful* [1 Cor. 4:1–2].

Calvin says, "The rule governing true stewardship is to carry out the duties faithfully." Certainly, negative and positive injunctions are to be carried out faithfully.

Probably the best illustration of this is seen in the following Scripture:

> *Look not every man on his own things, but every man also on the things of others.*
> *Let this mind be in you, which was also in Christ Jesus:*
> *Who, being in the form of God, thought it not robbery to be equal with God:*
> *But made himself of no reputation, and took upon him the form of a servant, and was made* (coming) *in the likeness of men:*

> *And being found in fashion* (appearance) *as a man, he humbled himself, and became obedient unto death, even the death of the cross.*
>
> *Wherefore God also hath highly exalted him, and given him a name which is above every name:*
>
> *That at the name of Jesus every knee should bow, of things* (those) *in heaven, and things* (those) *in earth, and things* (those) *under the earth;*
>
> *And that every tongue should confess that Jesus Christ is Lord, to the glory of God the Father* [Phil. 2:4–11].

Is there a finer example of laboring for others, of providing for the needy, of being a faithful steward, of denying self than Paul's description of our Lord Jesus in these eight verses from the second chapter of Philippians? He did not steal or take that which did not belong to Him. He labored and was a faithful steward. He was obedient to the negative and positive injunctions. He clearly understood the motivating reasons. He did all of these for the glory of God.

Can we strive to do less? The power is available. The question is, do we have the will, the commitment, and the desire? Do we put God first, or do we put ourselves first? Do we realize our days are numbered? Are our priorities according to the will of God? Do we hunger and thirst after righteousness? Do we seek knowledge and understanding of Him who is the Son of God, our Lord and Master?

If the answer to these questions is yes, then we will not only hear the injunctions and accept the reasons, we will go forth and do them.

> *Let him that stole steal no more: but rather let him labor, working with his hands the thing which is good, that he may have to give to him that needeth.*

Amen!

16

Communicating With Believers and Non-Believers

> *Let no corrupt communication proceed out of your mouth, but that which is good to the use of edifying, that it may minister grace unto the hearers* [Eph. 4:29].

Our focus is on specific truths, originating with our Lord and Master and taught by the Apostle Paul. When considering these teachings bear in mind the one central truth: Jesus Christ is the Son of God, our Lord and Saviour. He said, *I am the way, the truth, and the life* [John 14:6]. Therefore, we need to remind ourselves of certain basic truths.

> *THAT which was from the beginning, which we have heard, which we have seen with our eyes, which we have looked upon, and our hands have handled, of the Word of life;*
>
> *That which we have seen and heard declare we unto you, that ye also may have fellowship with us: and truly our fellowship is with the Father, and with his Son Jesus Christ* [1 John 1:1, 3].

The Apostle John says, *That which was from the beginning*. He makes that statement as a matter of fact. It is similar to the opening of his Gospel. However, he immediately brings in a personal testimony that, as we know, has never been refuted but only confirmed. He continues saying, in the personal vein, . . . *which we have heard, which we have seen with our eyes, which we have looked upon, and our hands have handled, of the Word of life* [1 John 1:1].

John states affirmatively, based upon his firsthand knowledge, that Christ was from the beginning. He affirms the *Word of life* and his witness to it by stating the experience of his three primary senses: he has heard, he has seen, and he has handled Him.

This first-person testimony and witness confirm not only John's faith but ours in the Gospel. He does not believe in some supposition, nor is he assenting to something told to him, but he is embracing a truth with a firm conviction and subscribing to it based on personal experience. The Apostle John pulls together many truths confirming the Gospel.

He states he is teaching what he thoroughly learned from the Master. His teachings are not based upon rumors, nor does he present them thoughtlessly. He says a person cannot be a fit teacher who has not first been a student of Jesus, learned from Him, and accepted the authority of His teachings. Oh, that teachers and preachers today would follow in his footsteps.

John continues by saying we have seen, we have beheld, and we have handled. The Apostle declares that he teaches nothing except that which was made known to him by the Master. John says that all his senses were employed and that he was able to comprehend Christ's power, authority, and teachings. Further, all of them were utilized for a period of time, both during Jesus' earthly ministry and after His resurrection. As John applied the power, the authority, and the teachings he grasped the reality of Christ, not only in his life, but in witnessing to others. Pray God we may enjoy the same experiences and do the same.

The Apostle John repeats *have seen* and *have heard* in the third verse. This substantiates the authority on which his teachings are based and provides the proper emphasis.

It is important to note at this juncture that Christ selected people to teach the Gospel who would be faithful witnesses. Those selected were motivated to have fellowship with one another in His name and to receive the blessings available from God through His Son. These factors had a significant impact not only in hearing the Word but in communicating it. They contributed immeasurably to increasing one's faith and witness and to applying the Master's teachings.

The Apostle John emphasizes that our fellowship is with the Father and the Son. He wants us to follow him as he leads us into a right relationship with God as members of Christ's body.

John says the disciples were adopted by Christ as members of His body, and so are we. We are to enjoy the fellowship and the relationship. Scripture says our joy in this fellowship is to be full. We are to be glad and joyful in our communion with God. It is to be the first and foremost thing in our minds. Consider, Matthew says, *Where your treasure is, there will your heart be also* [Matt. 6:21]. The psalmist says,

> *The Lord is the portion of mine inheritance and of my cup: . . .*
> *I have set the Lord always before me: . . .*
> *Therefore, my heart is glad, and my glory rejoiceth* [Ps. 16:5, 8–9].

Enjoying the fellowship means obeying God's commandments, hearing Christ's teachings, and pleasing Jesus by walking with Him. These truths apply to the teachings we are examining regarding Christlike conduct. We are to know and to apply the negative and positive injunctions plus understand the reason for each one.

The Apostle John continues by saying because we *have seen, have heard*, and *have handled*, we are to walk in the light not in the darkness. The reason we are to walk in the light is due to the message and promise we have of Him. Remember, Paul said to the Ephesians, *the truth is in Jesus* [Eph. 4:21]. When considering these teachings, bear in mind that it is because of Him, Him, Him, because we have seen Him, have heard Him, and have handled Him. Paul says to Titus, *For the grace of God that bringeth salvation hath appeared to all* men [Titus 2:11]. *Teaching us that, denying ungodliness and worldly lusts, we should live soberly, righteously, and godly, in this present world* (age) [Titus 2:12]. How do we do this? How are we to walk in the light?

By learning the teachings of the Lord Jesus Christ and applying them; and by realizing that "God does not communicate to us empty fiction," as John Calvin states with humor and emphasis.

Paul presents facts, truths, and reasons. We ignore them to our detriment and peril. There is nothing so insidious in the realm of Christendom, nothing so injurious to the body of Christ, nothing further from the teachings of Scripture, than the notion that adults do not have to study Christ's teachings and apply themselves to His teachings. No, that is not the teaching of our Master.

Unfortunately, ministers and teachers who do not proclaim the whole Gospel do much harm to furthering the witness of the Lord Jesus Christ and to presenting the truth to both the believer and the nonbeliever.

Let us turn our attention back to Ephesians: *Let no corrupt communication proceed out of your mouth, but that which is good to the use of edifying, that it may minister grace unto the hearers.* Again we have the negative, the positive, and the reason. In this verse, the Apostle addresses something common to all people, something that is part of everyday living. It is something that can be used to the glory of God and obedience to His will, or it can be ignored.

Speech and the type of speech are important. Paul mentions it several times in these passages:

> *... putting away lying*
> *Let no corrupt communication proceed out of your mouth,*
> *Let ... evil speaking, be put away from you,*
> *But fornication, and ... covetousness, let it not be once named among you as becometh saints* [Selections from Eph. 4:25, 29, 31, 5:3]

Obviously, according to the Apostle and the Holy Spirit a person's speech is a vital part of his or her life. Further, how their speech is applied and used should receive prominence and careful consideration when studying Scripture, and applying it to our daily living.

> *Let not sin therefore reign in your mortal body, that ye should obey it in the lusts thereof.*
> *Neither yield* (present) *ye your members as instruments* (weapons) *of unrighteousness unto sin: but yield* (present) *yourselves unto God, as those that are alive from the dead, and your members as instruments* (weapons) *of righteousness unto God* [Rom. 6:12–13].

One of man's instruments is speech. It is unique to man. This instrument, as well as the others given by God, is to be used to serve Him, it is not to be used against Him. "The fruit of the lips reveals the quality of the tree. Bad language and foul talk defile the whole man and manifest his corruption," Markus Barth tells us.

We are to serve God and Christ. Therefore, we are to control our speech. "Our conversation is to be used for the upbuilding of the body of Christ," as Ruth Paxson said. It is to be constructive, not destructive.

The tongue and language are two of our greatest gifts. How we use them reflects our relationship to God and the place He occupies in our lives. James accurately describes the impact that one's tongue and conversation have on him or her, and on others, when he says,

Communicating With Believers and Non-Believers

> *Even so the tongue is a little member, and boasteth great things. Behold, how great a matter* (forest) *a little fire kindleth* (sets on fire)*!*
>
> *And the tongue is a fire, a world of iniquity: so is the tongue* (set on fire) *among our members, that it defileth the whole body, and setteth on fire the course of nature* (existence)*; and it is set on fire of hell.*
>
> *For every kind of beasts, and of birds, and of serpents, and of things in the sea, is tamed, and hath been tamed of mankind:*
>
> *But the tongue can no man tame; it is an unruly evil, full of deadly poison* [Jas. 3:5–8].

The tongue has a great influence on one's life, whether as a hearer or as a speaker. It is important to control it and realize the impact speech can have on others as well as ourselves. Think about the reaction a few words can produce. Words that should not have been spoken, words that are misinterpreted.

Speech reveals what is in the heart, what a person is thinking. Also, it reveals the teachings of our Lord. Jesus was rather specific, and as we saw previously, He could be forthright and angry.

A person speaks out of the abundance of his or her heart or mind. What slips out or what is stated reveals much about a person. Therefore, it is not surprising that the Apostle Paul directs so much attention to this matter of speech.

Consider the Apostle's injunctions and reasons in some detail. First the negative one. *Let no corrupt communication proceed out of your mouth.* That is rather simple and straightforward. It means let no bad, foul, putrid, or defiling speech or language proceed out of your mouth. "Surely such speech should never fall from the lips of a Christian. Corrupt speech can be traced to one source: the unclean flow from an unclean fountain," as expressed by Ruth Paxson. That is not difficult to understand.

Paxson continues to expound upon this verse *Let no corrupt communication proceed . . . , but that which is good to the use of edifying, . . .* She says that . . . "God means for us to both control conversation so that it may not be along wrong lines, and to conduct it along those that are enobling and edifying. When we talk it is to be for a purpose,—*to minister grace unto the hearers.* This does not imply that conversation must always be on spiritual themes, certainly not just "pious" talk, nor necessarily that a complete ban is put on good humour and wholesome wit. But it does mean that it will be conversation that "becometh saints"; more than that, it will be such as befits the presence of the Holy Spirit who indwells us.

"The standard God has set for a walk in holiness is very high, but not unreasonable, because He has given to us the Holy Spirit to indwell and infill us for the very purpose of inworking into the spiritual fibre of our being the holiness of the Holy One."

Jesus spoke in parables and His disciples would ask Him to interpret the meaning of them. Also, he could speak directly and forcefully, as he did when he said,

> O generation (brood) *of vipers, how can ye, being evil, speak good things? for out of the abundance of the heart the mouth speaketh.*
> *A good man out of the good treasure of the heart bringeth forth good things: and an evil man out of the evil treasure bringeth forth evil things.*
> *But I say unto you, That every idle word that men shall speak, they shall give account thereof in the day of judgment.*
> *For by thy words thou shalt be justified, and by thy words thou shalt be condemned* [Matt. 12:34–37].

His words are clear and understandable in this passage from Matthew. They do not need to be interpreted. So be it!

What are the characteristics of corrupt communications? Usually they are marked by excesses and lack of control. It is when people talk too much and talk without thinking. Second, their conversations are usually an expression of self. It is self-centered, it focuses on self, it is selfish, and it exhibits or presents self first and foremost.

There is a desire on the part of these people to be interesting, entertaining, and admired. Much of their conversation is directed toward manifesting self and self-importance. These characteristics abound in the communications of those who are outside the body of Christ.

Third, corrupt communications are noted for their lack of delicacy or refinement. They are piquant or suggestive, unclean or foul, obscene or coarse, and vulgar or cutting. Able and intelligent people resort to this type of communication as well as less gifted people, and they do it for the reasons already stated.

Why do they do it? They do it for the oldest of reasons: sin, disobedience to the will of God. Putting self first, putting obedience to God second, third, fourth, or whatever.

There is another reason people resort to or use corrupt communications. Why? Because everybody is doing it. To communicate with people, to get down on their level, to talk so they will understand.

Others want to say it is acceptable. It is on television; it is in books, magazines, and articles. It is snickered about, and it is laughed about, but it is condoned.

What does the Apostle say? He says have nothing to do with it. This is based upon the teachings of the Master. This type of communication is corrupt in and of itself, and it corrupts others. Paul wants the members of Christ's body to realize that their language influences others. Therefore, they are to control it and refrain from injuring others.

What do corrupt communications do? They inflame, they arouse, they provoke, they corrupt, and they produce evil.

Therefore, the Apostle says do not let them proceed out of your mouth. Even if they enter your mind, even if the words begin to form in your mouth, do not utter them, stifle them. Do not let them hurt others or yourself.

We have looked at the negatives; now let's turn our attention to the positives. The Apostle says we are to speak, . . . *that which is good to the use of edifying, that it may minister grace unto the hearers* [Eph. 4:29]. What does the word *edifying* mean? It is translated from the Greek word *oikodomēo*, which means "to build up." This word is used in three different ways.

First, it signifies "to build up," whether it be figuratively or literally.

Second, it is used to promote the spiritual growth and development of believers by either teaching them or providing positive examples. It has an effect on local congregations. This is seen in Luke's account of Paul's visit to Caesarea and Tarsus.

> *Then had the churches rest throughout all Judea and Galilee and Samaria, and were edified; and walking in the fear of the Lord, and in the comfort of the Holy Ghost, were multiplied* [Acts 9:31].

> *He that speaketh in an unknown tongue edifieth himself; but he that prophesieth edifieth the church* [1 Cor. 14:4].

Also, it has an effect on individual believers and their actions.

> NOW as touching (concerning) *things offered unto idols, we know that we all have knowledge. Knowledge puffeth up, but charity* (love) *edifieth* (builds up) [1 Cor. 8:1]

> *All things are lawful for me, but all things are not expedient* (helpful)*: all things are lawful for me, but all things edify not* (do not build up) [1 Cor. 10:23].

> *For thou verily givest thanks well, but the other is not edified* [1 Cor. 14:17].

> *Wherefore comfort* (encourage) *yourselves* (each other) *together, and edify* (buildup) *one another, even as also ye do* (are doing) [1 Thess. 5:11].

These verses reveal that edification impacts others.

Third, it has an effect on the individual with regard to himself. We should note how the Revised Standard Version interprets this phrase. It says,

> *Let no evil talk come out of your mouths, but only such as is good for edifying, as fits the occasion, that it may impart grace to those who hear* [Eph. 4:29 RSV].

"This is probably a better translation: *Only such as is good for edifying* (and) . . . *as fits the occasion,*" as noted by Lloyd-Jones.

How meaningful is that teaching! Our verbal communications should be such that they are good for building up the body of Christ, others, and ourselves *as fits the occasion*.

Difficult? Think about that injunction. Think about Christ's teachings and how we communicate. Once we begin to grapple with the Master's teachings, we begin to see how weak we are, how we like to go around with our own mindsets, how we prefer to gloss over a lot of material, and how we ignore certain teachings.

Do you now see why the Apostle uses the term *walk* so frequently? We are to walk and talk; we are to learn what is important to the Master. You cannot do it if you go racing by.

What characteristics should be evident in the conversation of the members of Christ's body?

First, the believers' conversation should never be out of control. They should always be thinking about what they are saying and be responsible for it, since they will be held accountable for all their utterances.

The new man's conversation is to be in the light; it is not to be in the darkness. It is to be under control and conform to the commandments of God. It is to be according to the truth as it is in Jesus.

"Second, communications should not be selfish or self-centered. Actually, the conversation of the new man should show concern for other people," as proclaimed by Lloyd-Jones. As the Apostle says, *Speak every man truth with his neighbor* [Eph. 4:25]. Or, *BE YE ANGRY, AND SIN NOT; let not the sun go down upon your wrath* [Eph. 4:26]. We are not to be concerned with ourselves except *such as is good for edifying, as fits the occasion.*

We are to open our hearts and minds to the Lord Himself and to have His mind in us. Then we are to speak.

Third, our conversation is to be good! You will note the phrase says *Good to the use of edifying*, or in the Revised Standard Version *But only such as is good for edifying, as fits the occasion.*

"There is to be a purpose to the communication, some value or point to it," as appropriately expressed by Martyn Lloyd-Jones. It does not mean that we are always talking religion or that we don't laugh.

Fourth, it should *fit the occasion*. Again, this is difficult, but it is most important. We must consider with whom we are speaking and the situation at hand. The conversation should be appropriate for the circumstances. We should remember that wherever we are, we are witnessing to the Lord Jesus Christ. Also, people will notice that there is someone who calls himself or herself a Christian, someone who attends church regularly, and someone who listens to the Word of God that is being proclaimed, and it is having an effect on them.

Our conversation is to *fit the occasion*. It is not merely to reflect our own thoughts. We are not to pursue some topic just because we believe it is our duty to do so.

Sometimes the simplest conversations can be the most spirit-filled, and we may not even realize it. A genuine "How are you?" or "What have you been doing lately?" or "How is your wife?" may reveal a sincere regard for the other person and his/her interests; may fit the occasion. Surprisingly, such genuine communications may convey to another person God's own concern for him or her.

We are not to *cast pearls before swine* or give tough meat to babes. Paul says,

> *AND I, brethren, could not speak unto you as unto spiritual, but as unto carnal, even as unto babes in Christ.*
> *I have fed you with milk, and not with meat* (solid food): *for hitherto* (until now) *ye were not able to bear it, neither yet now are ye able* [1 Cor. 3:1–2].

"We are to learn to understand other people and their needs. And we should be so anxious to help them that we take time, we meditate, we think, we feel our way, we see the position and then we apply the necessary and appropriate word," as expressed by Martyn Lloyd-Jones.

It is utterly amazing how this works to the benefit of all when we take the time to pray to God for enlightenment, guidance, understanding, and the proper words before meeting with people, performing daily tasks, going to church, and all the other activities in which we may be engaged, and how God through the Holy Spirit will bless us and enlighten us.

This is difficult, this can tax us, and this takes practice, patience, and above all, understanding and wisdom; but then Jesus never promised to make it easy. Our communication is to be *good for edifying, as fits the occasion*. Therefore, we are to carefully select our words, our language, and our speech.

Why? So that our speech *may minister grace unto the hearers*. This does not mean that our speech is to charm the hearers, but that it is to *minister grace*. It is to show the way to God's grace and power and to demonstrate His grace. When it does *minister grace*, it should be seen in the greetings and in the conversation.

When it imparts God's grace it will do so to all the hearers who open and do not close their hearts and minds. God will help them acquire knowledge and understanding.

The example for our communications is to be the Master. We, like Him, come into contact with all sorts of people, with individuals who are weary, who are burdened, who are suffering, who do not have hope, who are lonely, who are disappointed, who are bitter, who are not friendly, and who are disillusioned.

Therefore, let us study the teachings of the Master, pray for guidance, and apply it, so that our conversation may *minister grace unto the hearers*. Our Lord came to do that. We are His disciples; therefore, we are to do as he would have us to do.

This means we are to select our words with care, whether they be words of cheer, words of encouragement, words of support, words of rebuke, words of correction, words of grace, or the words of Jesus. The Apostle Paul admonishes each of us with words that are direct and understandable saying, *Let no corrupt communication proceed out of your mouth, but that which is good to the use of edifying, that it may minister grace unto the hearers.*

Thank God that He enlightens us, challenges us, and wants us to be something—His disciples.

Amen!

17

Grieve Not the Holy Spirit

And grieve not the holy Spirit of God, whereby ye are sealed unto the day of redemption [Eph. 4:30].

Paul continually amazes me with his thoughts, his teachings, and the manner by which he presents the truths of our Lord Jesus Christ. We have examined negative injunctions, positive ones, and specific reasons for applying these truths, which are common to all and known by all the hearers of the Word.

Then, in the midst of these truths, he inserts a significant teaching regarding the Holy Spirit, who has been given to us by God through His Son. It is the Holy Spirit who dwells within us, and is part of the Holy Trinity. Paul commands, *And grieve not the holy Spirit of God* [Eph. 4:30]. That is a mighty exhortation!

Note the flow of Paul's teaching leading up to this command,

> *But, ye have not so learned Christ;*
> *As the truth is in Jesus;*
> *Put off . . . the old man, . . . put on the new man;*
> *Which after God is created in righteousness and true holiness*
> [Selections from Eph. 4:20–22, 24].

Then he presents prohibitions, commandments, and motivating factors regarding our conduct and our relationship to the Lord Jesus Christ.

> *Putting away lying, SPEAK EVERY MAN TRUTH WITH HIS NEIGHBOR;*
> *BE YE ANGRY AND SIN NOT;*
> *Steal no more; and*
> *Let no corrupt communication proceed out of your mouth, but that which is good to the use of edifying* [Selections from Eph. 4:25–26, 28–29].

After citing these things he says, *And grieve not the holy Spirit of God, whereby ye are sealed unto the day of redemption* [Eph. 4:30].

When considering this command, it is well to remember, as James Millard wrote, "Paul was writing to people he knew and they knew him, so he did not expand superfluously upon his words, but provided them with the essence of his teaching."

When our oldest granddaughter was three months old, I had the good fortune to spend a few minutes and unfortunately it was only 10–15 minutes with her. I carried her upstairs so I could talk to her as I packed my bag. The question came to mind, how could I or anyone grieve this child? How can anyone grieve a baby?

Then the larger question loomed before me. How can we who are members of the body of Christ grieve the Holy Spirit, who was sent by the Father to dwell with us after His Son, our Lord and Saviour, went to the Cross, bled, suffered, and died for your sins and mine? How can we grieve Him?

The Greek word Paul uses for *grieve* is *lupeō*. It means "to cause pain, grief, distress, sorrow to the Holy Spirit dwelling within us." It is both our actions and our thoughts that may grieve Him.

This particular verse comes after important truths have been enumerated but precedes the teachings contained in the next eight verses [Eph. 4:32–5:7]. It is the culmination of what has preceded it and prepares us for what follows.

What is the primary point Paul stresses in this fourth chapter? That we *put on the new man, which after* (according to) *God is created in righteousness and true holiness* [Eph. 4:24]. The emphasis should be on "according to God," not according to anyone or anything else, but "according to God"! Then Paul commands us in clear and concise words, *grieve not the holy Spirit of God* [Eph. 4:30].

Calvin provides additional insight regarding Paul's admonition to *grieve not the holy Spirit of God*, . . . saying, "[s]ince the Holy Spirit dwells in us, to Him every part of our soul and of our body ought to be consecrated. But if we give ourselves up to anything unclean, it is as if we drive Him away from His lodging. To express this more familiarly, he ascribes human affections, joy and grief, to the Holy Spirit. 'Endeavor, . . . that the Holy Spirit may dwell cheerfully in you, as in a pleasant and joyful dwelling, and give Him no occasion for grief.' . . . For godly ears not only dislike what is contrary to godliness, but are wounded with deep sorrow when it is heard."

There is an important point at this juncture. Scripture focuses its teachings upon God, the Lord Jesus Christ, and the Holy Spirit. Other teachings and religions may say do not steal, do not lie, do not be angry, do not use bad or foul language. They give various reasons for these injunctions, but having a right relationship with God and obeying His command to *grieve not the holy Spirit of God* is not among them [Eph. 4:30].

These are the distinguishing factors in Christ's teachings and in the reasons offered for doing certain things. Our thinking, conduct, behavior, and speech are to be based upon having a right relationship with God. If we have a right relationship with Him, then we are not going to grieve the Holy Spirit.

Paul makes it clear that when the Holy Spirit is grieved, it is not just God who suffers or is hurt. It is all those who are members of the body of Christ. We are not to sin against the Holy Spirit. This particular verse is unique in its context. It has a negative injunction, not a positive one. It states the reason for the prohibition. It contains truths at the heart of sanctification. It is not my intention to discuss the Doctrine of Sanctification at this time, but to expound upon this particular verse. We are concerned with the Apostle's command to *grieve not the holy Spirit of God*.

Paul is not appealing to a moral code or law, or to a statement of ethics, or to legal standards. All those things have their place. He is not saying we should do these things for our own benefit or that we should refrain from them for the same reason.

Paul tells us directly and forthrightly what is pleasing to God and what is not. As we have seen, the four sins of lying, anger, stealing, and corrupt communications, plus the commands regarding them, place demands upon us that are not easy. They are difficult. Now he adds a fifth injunction, *And grieve not the holy Spirit of God, whereby ye are sealed unto the day of redemption*. Again, this is difficult.

The Apostle makes it clear that our thoughts, actions, conduct, and behavior are to be the result of what Christ has done for us. We are to remember, . . . *as the truth is in Jesus* and . . . *which after God is created in righteousness and true holiness* [Eph. 4:21, 24].

Why are we to have a positive relationship with the Holy Spirit and not grieve Him? Our total life, every aspect of it, is to be lived in a joyful state. Jesus said, *I am come that they might have life, and that they might have it more abundantly* [John 10:10]. This requires the body being obedient to the Head, Jesus Christ, and the Spirit who is dwelling within us. We are not to grieve the Holy Spirit.

In the latter half of the fourth chapter, Paul gives explicit instructions as to how Christ's disciples are to walk, emphasizing that they are not to be disobedient to Christ's commands and teachings, nor walk *in the vanity* (futility) *of their mind(s)*. We are to learn, understand, and act accordingly. When we do, we please God; when we don't, we displease Him and grieve the Holy Spirit.

This verse [Eph. 4:30] contains a motivating reason for not grieving the Holy Spirit of God. By not grieving Him we *are sealed unto the day of redemption*. This admonition follows immediately after the three injunctions relating to lying, anger, and corrupt communications.

If the Spirit dwells within us, our speech should directly reflect His presence.

> *For it is not ye that speak, but the Spirit of your Father which speaketh in you* [Matt. 10:20].
>
> THE SPIRIT OF THE LORD IS UPON ME, BECAUSE HE HATH APPOINTED ME TO PREACH THE GOSPEL TO THE POOR (IN SPIRIT) [Luke 4:18].
>
> *And they were all filled with the Holy Ghost, and began to speak with other tongues, as the Spirit gave them utterance* [Acts 2:4].
>
> *He that hath an ear, let him hear what the Spirit saith unto the churches* [Rev. 2:7].

The Spirit enables men to attest to the truth and to witness to the Lord Jesus. The Spirit is grieved when we lie to one another or use corrupt communications. However, the Spirit rejoices when we speak the truth, especially as it is in Jesus, and when speaking that which is good for edifying and fits the occasion. We are to speak and to do those things that find favor with God and are acceptable to Him.

It is important to remember that the Holy Spirit dwells within us and that we have been sealed with Him. You will recall: *In whom ye also trusted, after that ye heard the word of truth, the gospel of your salvation: in whom also after that ye believed, ye were sealed with that holy Spirit of promise* [Eph. 1:13].

"Because God has sealed us by His Spirit, we vex Him when we do not follow His guidance, but pollute ourselves with ungodly passions.

No language can adequately express the gravity of this statement, that the Holy Spirit rejoices and is glad in us , when we are obedient to Him in all things, and neither think nor speak anything but what is pure and holy; and on the other hand, is grieved when we give place to anything that is unworthy of our calling. Now, let any man reckon what shocking ungodliness there is in piercing the Holy Spirit with such sorrow as to compel Him to withdraw from us at last. . . . For the Spirit of God is like a seal, by which we are distinguished from the reprobate, and which is impressed on our hearts that we may be assured of the grace of adoption," as revealed to John Calvin by the Holy Spirit.

Sealed with that holy Spirit reminds us of a significant fact: the Holy Spirit dwells within us, as is stressed throughout the New Testament.

> *But ye are not in the flesh, but in the Spirit, if so be that the Spirit of God dwell in you. Now if any man have not the Spirit of Christ, he is none of his.*
> *And if Christ be in you, the body is dead because of sin; but the Spirit is life because of righteousness.*
> *But if the Spirit of him that raised up Jesus from the dead dwell in you, he that raised up Christ from the dead shall also quicken* (give life to) *your mortal bodies by* (because of) *his Spirit that dwelleth in you* [Rom. 8:9–11].

"The distinguishing mark on the sons of God is the regeneration performed by the Holy Spirit dwelling within us," according to Calvin's wonderful, heart-warming description.

> *What? know ye not that your body is the temple of the Holy Ghost which is in you, which ye have of God, and ye are not your own?*
> *For ye are bought with a price: therefore glorify God in your body, and in your spirit, which are God's* [1 Cor. 6:19–20].

What should we do since we are temples and the Holy Spirit dwells within us? Every part of us is to be consecrated to Him. Conversely, if we give ourselves up to anything unclean, we are driving the Holy Spirit away from His dwelling place.

It is obligatory upon each of us to provide a dwelling place for the Holy Spirit that is pleasant and joyful and does not provide any cause for grieving Him. We are not to grieve the Holy Spirit that dwells within us individually and collectively as members of the body of Christ.

What should we remember about the Holy Spirit? That God is eternal in the Holy Trinity, the Father, Son, and Holy Ghost. He is independent of any and everything. He exists in Himself. He existed before time, before the world. He is not affected by us or what we do.

On the other hand, we are creatures of time, created, affected by other things and other events, and dependent. That is why we submit to lying, anger, stealing, corrupt communications, covetousness, and many other characteristics of the person who walks in darkness.

God is outside these things. He is above and beyond them. Yet we are told *grieve not the holy Spirit of God* [Eph. 4:30].

How do we reconcile these things? Our relationship to the Holy Spirit is one of love. If we love the Holy Spirit, then we should not grieve Him.

Our relationship to the Holy Spirit is personal, just as our relationship to the Lord Jesus is. Do not forget this: our relationship to each of them is personal.

What else should we remember? The Holy Spirit is a person; that is why we can grieve Him. We cannot grieve an influence, or a power, or a principle, or a thing. But we can grieve a person. We can grieve the Holy Spirit.

Who can grieve the Holy Spirit? The believers, the members of the body, not the unbelievers—they can only resist Him.

Think of family relations. A member of the family can grieve us by some word or action or by failing to do something. However, if some stranger acted the same way we would not be grieved. As members of a close-knit group we can grieve one another, whereas those who are not members would not grieve us.

We must constantly realize we are a dwelling place for the Holy Spirit, and due to His great love for us we can grieve Him by our words, thoughts, actions, and omissions.

How do we grieve the Holy Spirit? First, by the works of the flesh. Especially, as Paul pointedly states,

> *Now, the works of the flesh are manifest* (evident), *which are these; adultery, fornication, uncleanness, lasciviousness* (licentiousness),
> *Idolatry, witchcraft (sorcery), hatred, variance* (contentions), *emulations* (jealousies), *wrath, strife* (selfish ambitions), *seditions* (dissensions), *heresies,*
> *Envyings, murders, drunkenness, revellings, and such like: of the which I tell you before, as I have also told you in time past, that they which do such things shall not inherit the kingdom of God.* [Gal. 5:19–21].

Second, by our words, when we lie, or spew forth corrupt communications, or express anger unrighteously.

Third, by our thoughts as expressed in anger, jealousy, hatred, and envy, which are known to Him since He dwells within us.

Fourth, by ignoring Him. Is there anything more insulting, humiliating or depressing to someone than being ignored? The one thing I had better not do is to ignore my better half. It grieves someone to ignore them. Ask a mother, father, wife, husband, daughter, son, sister, or brother.

Fifth, by failing to respond to His influence, His leadings, and His promptings.

Sixth, by putting ourselves first and not doing those things, which will bless ourselves and others, but more importantly glorify God.

Why should we not grieve the Holy Spirit? Because of who He is. He is the third person in the Holy Trinity. It is safe to say our conduct would be according to God's will, if we realized every hour of every day that the Holy Spirit dwelled within us and that His love, power, and support were available at all times. We would still be able to perform all our tasks, enjoy ourselves, and partake of certain pleasures, but we would do it in a joyful manner. And we would obey Christ's commands and not be plagued by those injunctions against things that the Apostle wants us to discard or eliminate.

What else grieves the Holy Spirit? Our failure to understand the true objective of our salvation, which is not that our sins are forgiven, that life may be easy and without any hardships, or that all our problems will go away. No, it is not something that falls into these categories or similar ones.

The objective of our salvation is to glorify God and to have a right relationship with Him. It is stated concisely at the beginning of this letter, *According as he hath chosen us in him before the foundation of the world, that we should be holy and without blame before him in love* [Eph. 1:4]. How true!

The end of salvation is that we glorify Christ by becoming holy because of what He has done, not because of any works, contributions, or merit on our part.

Why did Christ die on the Cross? You can probably get many answers to that question. It is not because of His supreme act on the Cross, or that we will not go to Hell, or that our sins are forgiven. *It is for God's glory!* That we might have a right relationship with Him through Christ Jesus His Son.

The Apostle Peter says, *For if these things be in you* (are yours), *and abound, they make you that ye shall neither be barren* (useless) *nor unfruitful in the knowledge of our Lord Jesus Christ* [2 Pet. 1:8]. Think on that, we will be neither *barren nor unfruitful in the knowledge of . . . Christ.* Unfortunately, we may not know, or believe, or apply the teachings as received from Christ and His disciples. Instead, we may display ignorance and grieve the Holy Spirit of God.

If we continue to grieve the Holy Spirit, He will withdraw His presence from us. He may let us wander in the wilderness for forty years. It does not mean that He won't come back, but He may withhold His blessings. What happens when the Holy Spirit withholds His blessings or is absent? The spirit and flesh lust against each other.

Pray God that we will strive to walk in the Spirit and that we will grieve not the Holy Spirit of God. Further, that we will claim God's blessings and remember we are *sealed unto the day of redemption*. It is the very Spirit of God that seals us. We are to realize this, think about it, and apply it. May God give us the ability to remember it in the morning, evening, and at mid-day. We are not to grieve Him because to grieve Him is to grieve God. God has established a high and lofty standard for our walk in holiness with the Lord Jesus. However, it is not unreasonable. It may be difficult, and it may test us, but it is reasonable. Why?

Because the Holy Spirit dwells within us and fills us for the purpose of serving Him and being guided by Him. We are to take advantage of this and have our spiritual fiber filled each day. We are to be new wine. We are to walk with Him.

Thank God, Paul went to the heart of the matter and said to us, *And grieve not the holy Spirit of God, whereby ye are sealed unto the day of redemption* [Eph. 4:30].

Amen!

18

A Walk in Love

> *Let all bitterness, and wrath, and anger, and clamor, and evil speaking, be put away from you, with all malice:*
> *And be ye kind one to another, tenderhearted, forgiving one another, even as God for Christ's sake hath forgiven you*
> [Eph. 4:31–32].

The Holy Spirit works! He works through people. He works through us. He worked through the apostles. Their teachings support and amplify upon each other and the earthly ministry of our Lord and Master.

The Apostle Paul begins this fourth chapter saying, *I THEREFORE, the prisoner of* (in) *the Lord, beseech you that ye walk worthy of the vocation* (calling) *wherewith ye are called* [Eph. 4:1]. Since then we have been walking through Ephesians and applying those teachings on the path God has chosen. When straying from the right road, they provide the light to return to the Way and walk with the Lord. As we know, it is not easy, but it is beneficial and rewarding. It is where we have been called to walk, and when walking there, we are going in the right direction and traveling with the best company—the Master Himself.

Since the beginning of this fourth chapter, our journey has been marked by walking in unity and holiness. Now, we come to a third characteristic of this walk, walking in love.

The Apostle in these verses returns to presenting his teaching with a positive injunction, a negative one, and a motivating reason. First the negative, *Let all bitterness, and wrath, and anger, and clamor, and evil speaking, be put away from you, with all malice.* Next the positive, *And be ye kind one to another, tenderhearted, forgiving one another.* Then the motivating reason, *even as God for Christ's sake hath forgiven* (in Christ forgave) *you.*

Most preachers and teachers think about the Easter message for several weeks before the actual day. They pray that the Holy Sprit will work within them and guide them to proclaim God's truth and love. It is amazing how the Holy Spirit provides and makes available material appropriate for that occasion. If we are to proclaim God's truth and walk with Him in love, then we must know the terrain to be covered: what it encompasses; what we are to take with us; what we are to discard; and what to *put off*; and what to *put on* so there will be no void.

When proceeding on this walk we are to be concerned with the weightier matters of life. Jesus explicitly states what He means, saying,

> *Woe unto you, scribes and Pharisees, hypocrites! for ye pay tithe of mint and anise and cummin, and have omitted* (neglected) *the weightier matters of the law, judgment* (justice), *mercy, and faith: these ought ye to have done, and not to leave the other undone* [Matt. 23:23].

Faith in this verse means a firm conviction of God's truth as it has been revealed, a personal surrender to Him [John 1:12], and conduct inspired by such a surrender. What a difference Scripture makes when we understand the context and the meaning of the words used!

John's first Epistle may help us better understand and appreciate Paul's message in verses 31–32 of the fourth chapter of Ephesians, plus the new and old commandments he emphasizes. John says,

> *... an old commandment which ye had from the beginning. The old commandment is the word which ye have heard from the beginning.*
> *... a new commandment I write unto you, which thing is true in him and in you: because the darkness is past* (passing away), *and the true light now shineth* [1 John 2:7–8].

> *He that loveth his brother abideth in the light, and there is none occasion of* (no cause for) *stumbling in him.*
> *But he that hateth his brother is in darkness, ... and knoweth not whither he goeth, because that darkness hath blinded his eyes* [1 John 2:10–11].

These passages bear a direct relationship to characteristics that are prominent in our daily living: love and hate; and light and darkness. We are to understand these things according to the Gospel and according to God, not according to our earthly, secular mindsets.

John adds to these meaningful words saying,

> ... *whoso hath this world's good* (goods), *and seeth his brother have need, and shutteth his bowels* (heart) *of compassion from him, how dwelleth the love of God in him?*
> *My little children, let us not love in word, neither in tongue; but in deed and in truth* [1 John 3:17–18].

John's comments are based upon an extremely important teaching: to love God is to be evidenced by keeping His commandments. Therefore, we are to know them and to apply them.

John states that what he teaches about love is not new, but what the believers had heard from the beginning, even though it may now be considered old by some. The reason John calls it old is not only because of the antiquity of this teaching, but because the individual believers had been taught this from the time they first became members of Christ's body. John emphasizes that it comes from Christ Himself.

The Gospel should be received as proceeding from God and as His eternal truth, certainly not as something that is new or old. It is refreshing and vitalizing to see the sun come up in the morning or to receive needed rain. We are not to look on them as being old or antiques.

The truths of the Gospel are given as a holy rule or guide to living an abundant and joyful life. We are to remember that they are given through Christ, they are prescribed by Him, and they are affirmed and attested to by Him.

When John says *a new commandment*, what does he mean? God renews it each day, by reminding us of it. He wants us to practice it. He realizes our general welfare, and our relationship to Him depends upon it.

Further, if we are to make progress in living, then we must make progress in knowing the love of God in Christ Jesus. The truth that is in Christ is also in us. However, that does not mean we have complete knowledge when we become members of His body, or have been members for a period of time.

Paul's statement to the Philippians should help us to understand this truth.

> *Not as though I had already attained, either were already perfect: but I follow after, if that I may apprehend that for which also I am apprehended of Christ Jesus.*
>
> *Brethren, I count not myself to have apprehended: but this one thing I do, forgetting those things which are behind, and reaching forth unto those things which are before* [Phil. 3:12–13].

The Apostle Paul was extremely desirous of apprehending and thoroughly receiving Christ Jesus and the truth that is in Him. He wanted to take possession of it because of its beneficial effect. He wanted to lay hold of it with his mind and understanding so that he could perceive both the light and darkness as revealed by the Lord Jesus Christ.

Paul realized above everything else that daily progress is necessary. The sun cannot reach noonday nor can it set until it first rises. It is the same sun that rises each day. We are to advance in the love of God each day so that we may be filled for each opportunity presented to us.

What does John say about love in his first Epistle? First, love is the primary rule or guide by which our life is to be tested. Note, it will be tested. Second, those who are strangers to love are blind and walk around in darkness. To whom does this statement apply? To those who are strangers to the love of God and to the love of their neighbors. It is based upon God's teachings, not on our own experiences, thoughts, or desires.

It is easy to say we love God, especially when everything goes our way. However, it may seem onerous when we realize that we must obey His commandments, change our mindsets, love our neighbor, and pray for our adversaries.

God prepares us to do these things, but we resist them. It appears we resist four interrelated commandments more than any others:

> *THOU SHALT LOVE THE LORD THY GOD WITH ALL THY HEART, AND WITH ALL THY SOUL, AND WITH ALL THY MIND* [Matt. 22:37].

> *THOU SHALT LOVE THY NEIGHBOR AS THYSELF* [Matt. 22:39].

> *That ye love one another; as I have loved you, that ye also love one another* [John 13:34].

> *If ye love me, keep my commandments.* [John 14:15]

Yes, we say we love Him, and I am sure we do to a certain extent. I am sure the disciples liked and possibly loved Jesus when they first were called to follow Him, but I am more than confident that their initial love paled in comparison to the love they experienced at the end of His ministry, after the resurrection, and after Pentecost.

How impressive it is that John, in his sunset years, could vividly remember and record the Master's words,

> He that hath my commandments, and keepeth them, he it is that loveth me: and he that loveth me shall be loved of my Father, and I will love him, and will manifest (reveal) myself to him
> [John 14:21].

Also he recorded,

> If ye keep my commandments, ye shall abide in my love; even as I have kept my Father's commandments, and abide in His love [John 15:10].

Because of these truths John wrote,

> We know that we have passed from death unto life, because we love the brethren. He that loveth not his brother abideth in death. Whosoever hateth his brother is a murderer [1 John 3:14–15].

"Love is the special fruit of the Spirit, it is also a sure symbol of regeneration," John Calvin wrote with joy in his heart.

A person does not sincerely love his brother or sister unless he or she is born again by God's Spirit and the Spirit dwells within him or her. The love comes first and then the life. The order is not reversed.

Therefore, with this background, let us turn our attention back to Ephesians 4:31–32. The negative injunction focuses on six specific sins: bitterness, wrath, anger, clamor, evil speaking, and malice. These are all common maladies. But they are ones we like to skim over, not dwell upon. "Here we see Satan's brood hatched out in the nest of hate into concrete sins of temper and tongue. Let us note several things. First, unlove is the setting for all six sins mentioned here. Not one of them could abide in a love-filled, love-constrained heart. Secondly, there is a gradation in the expression of unlove from an inner attitude to an outward act," as stated by Ruth Paxson.

There is another trait common to these sins: the setting for each of them is unlove. They cannot reside, let alone grow, in a heart that is filled with God's love or constrained by it. Plus, an expression of unlove springs from within a person. The action is the result of an inner attitude. It originates as the result of some act or word that develops into resentment or bitterness. It is nursed until it produces and exhibits the other sins listed by the Apostle.

Let us look at each of these sins. *Bitterness* is from the Greek word *pikria*, which denotes "bitterness" or, in this verse, "bitter hatred." It is expressed in people by persistent sourness or the lack of amiability. It is an unloving condition and does not see any good in anything.

Paxson elaborates on the first hateful expression stating that "[t]hat root of "bitterness," canker in the innermost spirit, or secret resentment over some hurt or wrong, allowed to home itself in the heart, will one day flame into white heat in an outburst of passionate fury. That grievance nursed in the spirit, that indignation which became a settled attitude of mind, that hot feeling of injury which smoulders in the heart will one day reach the tongue and find expression in heated discussion, "clamour," and intemperate "evil speaking." Lastly, there is an inevitable progress in unlove if left unchecked."

What makes people bitter? Normally, they ponder or meditate upon grievances or misfortunes. As a result they degenerate into a state of bitterness. This is true of both real and imaginary grievances. Bitterness describes a life that has gone sour. I can not help but think of Robert E. Lee, who upon learning of their child's death wrote to Mrs. Lee expressing the hope that she, too, may accept the will of God with a right heart.

The second and third sins Paul identifies are *wrath* and *anger*. Wrath means "hot anger" or "passion." The Greek word for wrath is *thumos*. It indicates "an agitated condition of the feelings." It is an outburst from "an inward indignation." *Anger*, on the other hand, is from the Greek word *orgē* which suggests "a more settled or abiding state of mind, but one with a view towards revenge." *Anger* in this instance is less volatile in being expressed, but it is more lasting in its nature. Wrath expresses an inward feeling, while anger is a more active emotion. Wrath is seen in violent excitement and in an agitating mind, while anger is a more settled state. The fourth and fifth sins identified are *clamor* and *evil speaking*. *Clamor* is the tumult of controversy. It is evident in brawling, shouting, and violence. It is a repugnant and terrible thing. It should never be seen in a member of Christ's body. Evil speaking means clearly and deliberately saying things that are injurious to others. It is saying or repeating things calculated to harm others.

Paul, under the influence of the Holy Spirit, is saying this to the members of Christ's body. Think of the harm that evil speaking does. Think of its impact upon families, relations, congregations, and communities. Think of the lives and relations it has ruined. "A devil touched, hate tipped tongue will go to any length of railing, slander, insult, and abuse in giving vent to anger," as vividly expressed by Ruth Paxson. This is not to be exhibited by a Christian.

Last, we have *malice*. What is it? It expresses itself through ill will and a determination to harm others. It is an infection that infests a person and controls him or her in such a way that he or she seeks to injure others; malice does not rest until it works some evil. The henchman of hate is malice.

Note the progression the Apostle uses: from bitterness, which originates internally; to wrath and anger, which are conditions resulting from a grievance or resentment; to clamor and evil speaking, which are outward expressions; to malice, which occurs and becomes a state of mind and heart occasionally, frequently, or permanently.

When these sins are present there is unlove. The Apostles John and Paul know it. So what does Paul say? *Let all* of these six sins *be put away from you.* You have to reject them when they first appear, or you have to kick them out when they take up residence, even if it is only for a few minutes.

Again and again it comes back to the little words in Scripture that are so important. Paul says *Let all*. The word *let* places the responsibility squarely on the shoulders of each one of us, as well as in our minds and hearts, to do something. It is something we cannot duck or sidestep. This is our responsibility, and it requires exercising self-control. There are no acceptable excuses. Why? Because the power is available from the Lord Jesus through the Holy Spirit, and we are to take specific action.

Next, is the word *all*. It is probably the biggest word in the whole verse. It means all, any, every particle, kind, or variety. Not only are *all* of these sins to be removed, but every little trace of them. They are to be swept clean. If not, they will fester and grow, and become evident once again.

"There is to be no root of bitterness, no symptom of wrath, no trace of anger, no echo of clamor, no slime of evil speaking and no dregs of malice" remaining in a person, nor seen in one's conduct at any time or place, as Ruth Paxson says of this verse. Is that plain enough and sufficiently direct?

Now do you believe it when someone says it is easy to be a Christian? The progression of faith is easy, but the obeying, doing, and practicing are extremely difficult. It requires effort, prayer, and self-control, and more of the same on a continuing basis.

If there is any trace of those sins within us, the Holy Spirit is grieved and we are told to *grieve not the holy Spirit of God* [Eph. 4:30]. Evidence of these sins is not only against the will of God, it also reveals the absence of love. Our conduct as members of the body is not merely based upon a list of "thou shalt nots," or getting rid of the sins of the flesh and mind, but on exercising extreme care to fill our hearts and minds with the love of God in Christ Jesus: to *put off* the old and *put on* the new.

We must realize that even though we are members of Christ's body, it does not mean that all our troubles have disappeared and will never beset us in the future.

So much for the negative injunction. Let's focus on the positive. You cannot deal with the negative unless you are dealing with the positive at the same point in time. We are to consider them concurrently.

My wife fusses about the oak leaves on our patio during the springtime. They fall continuously, and at times sound like falling rain. Yet the tree never becomes barren. What happens? The new leaves appear and push off the old ones. The old is pushed off the branches to make way for the new.

The positive commandment begins with the words *be ye kind*. What the Apostle actually wrote was "become ye kind." These words suggest a process, not an accomplished fact. It is something to be cultivated. It does not just happen, nor does it happen automatically. You do not receive it at any one moment in time.

To become kind is more than doing kindly deeds. It is understood only as we comprehend the kindness and love of our Lord and Saviour. "How kind the Lord Jesus is! Loving the unloving and the unlovable with a love that took Him to Calvary's Cross! It was also a kindness that in His earthly life made Him unfailingly courteous, considerate, appreciative, and thoughtful of others," as expressed with admiration and affection by Ruth Paxson.

We are to become kind even as He was kind. We are to progress, day by day, week by week and year by year. To be or to become kind is the opposite of being bitter. When we are kind we are useful and helpful to others.

Next, we are to become tenderhearted. Our hearts are to respond, move, and act as Christ would have us to do. "How strange it is that it is much easier to be harshly uncharitable and intolerant than to be sympathetic, loving and understanding! Could we be aught but tender-hearted if we ever kept Christ on Calvary in our vision? Would our heart not be kept full of compassion toward others who have shortcomings and sins if we remembered what we were and always would have been but for the love of God manifested toward us in Christ?" This food for thought is provided by Ruth Paxson.

Is it not strange and confusing that people can be harsh, uncharitable, and intolerant so easily, yet it is difficult for them to become loving, understanding, compassionate, kind, and tenderhearted? Peter says,

> *Finally, be ye all of one mind, having compassion one of another, love as brethren, be pitiful* (tenderhearted), *be courteous:*
> *Not rendering evil for evil, or railing* (reviling) *for railing* (reviling)*: but contrariwise blessing; knowing that ye are thereunto called, that ye should inherit a blessing* [1 Pet. 3:8–9].

The word *pitiful* in this verse should be translated as "tenderhearted." It means that we are to help our brethren by doing what we can to relieve their miseries and to help them bear their infirmities. As the two apostles proclaim, we are to become tenderhearted.

The third positive injunction is that we are to become forgiving. Note the progression Paul uses: become kind, then become tenderhearted, and then become forgiving. If a person becomes the first two, then the third should follow. Forgiving is at the opposite end of the spectrum from malice.

Paul says *forgiving one another*. Some people misunderstand or misinterpret Christ's teachings. They ignore, or overlook, or refuse to see any wrong in anyone, and then say that is what we are to do. That is not the teaching!

We are to be realistic. We are to recognize and acknowledge the sin or sins committed by others. Then we are to forgive them, especially when they ask for forgiveness. We are not to pretend or fantasize that they have done nothing. Nor are we to allow grievances or resentments to fester into malice. No, but we are to forgive and to forget! Especially when someone truly asks for forgiveness.

What more is required of us? We are to forgive readily and freely, before the sun goes down. Difficult? You better believe it! That is why we read, obtain knowledge and understanding, and above all receive the power of the Holy Spirit and the love of God in Christ Jesus.

Yes, we are to become kind, tenderhearted, and forgiving! The natural question is, why? The Apostle provides the reason with simple and direct words saying, *even as God for Christ's sake hath forgiven* (in Christ forgave) *you* [Eph. 4:32].

Paxson provides additional clarity to Paul's command . . . *forgiving one another, even as God for Christ's sake hath forgiven you,* declaring, "[i]s it possible for unforgiveness to abide in the heart where kindness and tenderheartedness are dominant? The Christlike attitude results in the Christlike act. Is there any member of the Body of Christ whom you have not forgiven? If so, how can you hold out against the appeal God makes here?"

Can we truly argue with that reason? The psalmist says, *Bless the Lord, O my soul, and forget not all his benefits.* And the first benefit stated is, *Who forgiveth all thine iniquities; who healeth all thy diseases* [Ps. 103:2-3]. Please note an important point: Scripture says, *as God for Christ's sake hath forgiven* (in Christ forgave) *you* [Eph. 4:32]. It is not that He is going to forgive you, but that He already has. The people who carry out the positive injunctions are those who know that God has forgiven them. All the doubt has been removed from their hearts and minds.

Therefore, three questions are appropriate at this time:

- Do you know your sins have been forgiven?
- Does the exhortation to become kind, tenderhearted, and forgiving appeal to you?
- Is it desirable, or not?

The answers to these questions are vital. They tell much about your relationship to the Lord Jesus Christ.

Pray God we understand fully and completely the way in which God has forgiven us. It is *for Christ's sake.* He has done it in Christ because that is the only way it can be done. No one should say they rely upon God's love only for the forgiveness of sins. They should rely upon Him for so much more. He forgives our sins in spite of ourselves, not because of anything we may have done or might do. It is the free gift of God. He bestowed it upon us because of His love, His grace, His mercy, His compassion, His kindness, and His tenderheartedness.

He hath laid on Him the iniquity of us all. God has taken our sins and placed them on the Lord Jesus Christ and sent Him to the Cross that we might be forgiven.

When viewed in the light of this truth we should put away all the identified sins and become *kind, tenderhearted, forgiving one another. Why? . . . even as God for Christ's sake hath forgiven* (in Christ forgave) *you* [Eph. 4:32].

Yes, Christ went to the Cross that our sins might be forgiven. What about us? What are we to do? We are called to follow Christ as we proceed along life's journey. It is not easy, it requires increasing in faith, being steadfast in our faith, practicing the commands and teachings of Christ and not walking as other Gentiles (secularists) walk.

As we conclude this section, Following Christ, may we ponder the profound, uplifting,and strengthening words of that great hymn, "Jesus Calls Us" by the remarkable Frances Alexander:

Jesus call us: o'er the tumult
Of our life's wild restless sea,
Day by day His sweet voice soundeth,
Saying, "Christian, follow Me."

Jesus call us from the worship
Of the vain world's golden store,
From each idol that would keep us,
Saying, "Christian, love Me more."

In our joys and in our sorrows,
Days of toil and hours of ease,
Still He calls, in cares and pleasures,
"Christian, love Me more than these."

Jesus calls us: by Thy mercies,
Saviour, may we hear Thy call,
Give our hearts to Thine obedience,
Serve and love Thee best of all. A-Men

Amen!

Outline Questions

Chapter 1

WALK NOT AS OTHER GENTILES

This I say therefore, and testify in the Lord, that ye henceforth walk not as other Gentiles walk, in the vanity (futility) of their mind,

Having the understanding darkened, being alienated from the life of God through the ignorance that is in them, because of the blindness (hardening) of their heart:

Who being past feeling have given themselves over unto lasciviousness (licentiousness), to work all uncleanness with greediness [Eph. 4:17–19].

What five essential points are evident in the first sixteen verses of the fourth chapter?

What does our new position *in Christ* require?

What does the *blood of Christ* do for us?

How does the sinner become a saint?

What are we not to do when called to walk in the newness of life?

How does Paul speak to us?

What should a member of Christ's body consider as he or she continues to walk through Ephesians with the Lord Jesus?

What is *not* meant when a person begins to grow *in Christ*?

How is Christian righteousness obtained?

What is the difference between morality and Christian living?

How does the true growth and development of the Spirit's fruit occur?

What is at the center of the coin that has doctrine on one side and application on the other?

Upon what is the teaching of sanctification based?

With what should we be concerned as members of Christ's body?

Chapter 2

THE VANITY (FUTILITY) OF THEIR MIND

> *This I say therefore, and testify in the Lord, that ye henceforth walk not as other Gentiles walk, in the vanity (futility) of their mind, . . .* [Eph. 4:17].

Why does Paul emphasize that salvation is to be sought in the Gospel?

What do Paul and Ezekiel say about pastors and teachers proclaiming God's Word?

What privilege and duty does one have in preaching or teaching the Gospel?

How do we offend God?

What does Paul mean when he says, *that ye henceforth walk not as other Gentiles walk*?

What does Paul mean when he says, *I . . . testify in the Lord*?

What does the word *henceforth* mean in the original Greek?

Why does Paul, at times, stress negatives?

Where must you begin in order to change people or conditions?

What is the result of unfaithfulness?

Why has there been a decline in moral behavior in recent years?

What are we to do regarding evil?

What does the Greek word for *vanity* mean?

What was the outlook of the ancient world regarding life, death, and God?

What is the Apostle Paul saying to Christian believers?

Chapter 3

HARDNESS OF THEIR HEARTS

> *This I say therefore, and testify in the Lord, that ye henceforth walk not as other Gentiles walk, in the vanity* (futility) *of their mind,* . . . [Eph. 4:17].

Why are we to walk in the light?

What causes vanity or empty headedness?

Why are people estranged from God?

What are the results of ignoring God's teachings?

What does the Greek word for blindness really mean?

Why do people live in ignorance, darkness, and blindness, alienated from God?

What is the fundamental business of preaching and teaching?

Why do people disparage the Bible, despise it, or misunderstand it?

What does Paul stress to the Corinthians, Ephesians, and us regarding the Spirit of God?

Why is the spiritual man endowed with so much light?

When is a person able to judge correctly?

To whom is Paul speaking when he says, *But we have the mind of Christ*?

How does Paul's prayer at the end of the third chapter apply to us?

What can remove the darkness and provide light?

For what are we to pray?

Chapter 4

ALIENATED FROM GOD

> *This I say therefore, and testify in the Lord, that ye henceforth walk not as other Gentiles walk, in the vanity* (futility) *of their mind,*
>
> *Having the understanding darkened, being alienated from the life of God through the ignorance that is in them, because of the blindness* (hardening) *of their heart:*
>
> *Who being past feeling have given themselves over unto lasciviousness* (licentiousness), *to work all uncleanness with greediness* [Eph. 4:17–19].

Where does the Apostle focus attention in his remarkable analysis?

What is the definition of life according to the Greek word *zoē*?

What is meant by the life of God?

What are the three degrees of life in this world?

What powers produce the regenerated life in Christ?

Why is a person alienated from God?

What happens to the person alienated from God?

Of what are men ignorant regarding God, His attributes, love, and power?

Why are we to stress knowing God and Christ?

What is meant by *being past feeling*?

What did Paul mean when he said, *Having their conscience seared with a hot iron*?

What factors contribute to the condition of *being past feeling*?

What does Paul mean when he says that they have *given themselves*?

What do the words *with greediness* include as used by Paul?

What teachings can impair the power of the church?

How does Paul describe the life of those alienated from God?

What questions are we to answer in the positive before proceeding?

Chapter 5

CONTRASTS: IN CHRIST—OUTSIDE CHRIST

> *But ye have not so learned Christ;*
> *If so be that ye have heard him, and have been taught by him, as the truth is in Jesus:*
> *That ye put off concerning the former conversation (conduct) the old man, which is corrupt according to the deceitful lusts;*
> *And be renewed in the spirit of your mind;*
> *And that ye put on the new man, which after God is created in righteousness and true holiness* [Eph. 4:20–24].

How do we learn Christ?

What did Luke reveal about the early followers?

What characteristics did Paul exhibit in teaching the Ephesians?

What does a sound and thorough instruction require of preachers and teachers?

How and when did Paul teach the Ephesians?

What type presentation is required from Christ's servants?

Outline Questions

Why did Paul stress repentance and faith?

What is the essence of reconciliation with God?

What ideas does Paul express when saying, *But ye have not so learned Christ*?

What does Paul mean when he says, *Christ speaking in me*?

What is the ultimate objective of Paul's teaching?

How does the Gospel come to us?

What is significant regarding conditions early in the twenty-first century?

What is the power of God able to do?

What does the person who is in Christ know?

How are we to act when we learn Christ?

What is Paul saying to the Ephesians and us?

Chapter 6

KNOWING THE TRUTH: HEARING AND LEARNING CHRIST

> *But ye have not so learned Christ;*
> *If so be that ye have heard him, and have been taught by him, as the truth is in Jesus* [Eph. 4:20–21].

What does learning Jesus require?

What is the key to living one's life in Christ?

How do we acquire knowledge, learning, understanding, and practical experience?

How are we to come unto a *knowledge of the truth*?

Why are we to think about our relationship to God?

What is required to *give an answer to every man that asketh you a reason of the hope that is in you*?

What is the most glorious thing we can learn?

To whom does God give spiritual insight?

Outline Questions 179

What impact does learning Christ have on a person?

Why do people change?

What is meant by the phrase *the truth as in Jesus*?

What does the truth that is in Jesus include?

What is the Apostle saying to the Ephesians in these verses?

Chapter 7

GOD'S AMAZING GRACE

> *That ye put off concerning the former conversation* (conduct) *the old man, which is corrupt according to the deceitful lusts;*
> *And be renewed in the spirit of your mind;*
> *And that ye put on the new man, which after God is created in righteousness and true holiness* [Eph. 4:22–24].

What do you find compelling in the words of the hymn *Amazing Grace*?

What contrasts does Paul use in these verses?

What important factors are presented?

How does Ruth Paxson describe these verses?

What is Paul telling us regarding *the old man* and *the new man*?

What do the clothing metaphors indicate?

What is the new man to become?

What is required to become a new creature in Christ's kingdom?

What are we to realize and give thanks for when we are reconciled to God?

How does reconciliation come?

Why is a person to put off and put on at the same time?

What are our responsibilities in putting off *the old man*?

What do the two natures within us require?

What does Paul exhort the Colossians to do?

What are we to *put on the new man*?

Why are we to be like new wineskins?

What should we remember each day?

Chapter 8

CORRUPT THROUGH THE LUSTS OF DECEIT

> *That ye put off concerning the former conversation* (conduct) *the old man, which is corrupt according to the deceitful lusts; And be renewed in the spirit of your mind; And that ye put on the new man, which after God is created in righteousness and true holiness* [Eph. 4:22-24].

What are the two natures in every saint?

With whom is our fellowship to be?

What is the bond of our union with God?

What does Christ provide that enables us to *put off . . . the old man*?

What are the negatives and positives regarding *desire* and *lust*?

What knowledge are we to have with respect to deceit?

What is significant about the natural instincts with which God has endowed man?

What does deceit do to a man?

How does Peter describe the outcome of evil lusts?

What is that type of life like?

What happens to those people?

What has been the story of the *father of lies* from the beginning?

Why does the author of the letter to the Hebrews warn us against hardening our hearts?

How does sin deceive us?

What is it that sin and deceit can never give?

Chapter 9

THE POWER OF GOD

> *That ye put off concerning the former conversation* (conduct) *the old man, which is corrupt according to the deceitful lusts;*
> *And be renewed in the spirit of your mind;*
> *And that ye put on the new man, which after God is created in righteousness and true holiness* [Eph. 4:22–24].

What does Paul want the Ephesians to know?

For what does Paul pray to God on behalf of the Ephesians?

What has Paul presented prior to issuing his command to put off the old and to put on the new?

To whom does Paul say to *put off . . . the old man . . .* [*a*]*nd that ye put on the new man*?

What do Scripture and the Holy Ghost do for us regarding putting *off the old man* and putting *on the new man*?

What false teaching has been propagated for many years about going to God in prayer?

Outline Questions 185

What does Paul have to say about this?

What happens when you bypass Scripture?

When does God command us?

How are we to act after receiving a command from God?

What is our behavior to become?

What external actions are we to exhibit?

What is our conversation and conduct to reflect?

What happened to the man with large mustaches?

What are we to do regarding the works of darkness?

Of what does Paul remind us regarding the needs of the flesh?

Why are we to mortify the flesh?

What happens when there is no confidence in God?

What does "*mortify* (put to death) *the deeds of the body*" mean?

Chapter 10

CONTROLLED BY THE SPIRIT OF CHRIST

And be renewed in the spirit of your mind; . . . [Eph. 4:23].

What profoundly changed Paul after his conversion?

What tasks were appointed to Paul?

What is required to *put off . . . the old man . . .* [a]*nd that ye put on the new man*?

What does Jesus say we are to do?

Why did Jesus say these things?

What does Jesus share with us?

What does it mean to *be renewed in the spirit of your mind*?

What is the key to the whole Bible?

Why do we emphasize being *renewed in the spirit of your mind*?

What needs to be done when the mind goes astray?

What happens to us when we are continuously renewed in the spirit of our minds?

Chapter 11

CREATED IN RIGHTEOUSNESS

> *And that ye put on the new man, which after God is created in righteousness and true holiness* [Eph. 4:24].

How is the *new man* created?

What two commandments does the person in Christ receive?

What are we to do and not to do?

What characteristics does Paul encourage the Corinthians to exhibit in their daily lives?

What contrasts does Paul emphasize?

Why does Paul stress *Be ye not unequally yoked together with unbelievers*?

How are we to conduct ourselves when we are the victims of attacks, insults, and innuendos?

What command did God give to Abram?

What does Paul mean by the terms *righteousness*, *holiness*, and *truth*?

How did Abraham obtain righteousness?

What does holiness involve?

What two characteristics is the new man to put on?

What is meant by the word *truth* when Paul says, *as the truth is in Jesus*?

After what are we to strive?

Chapter 12

TRUTH ACCORDING TO GOD

> *And that ye put on the new man, which after God is created in righteousness and true holiness* [Eph. 4:24].

What *truth* does God reveal about Himself and the Lord Jesus Christ?

Why does the Lord Jesus emphasize *truth*?

What does God demand of man regarding *the truth*?

How is *truth* stated in the New Testament?

Why is there so much emphasis on *the truth* in Jesus?

What happens as a result of a knowledge of *the truth*?

What is the purpose of the Gospel and the object of salvation?

What does this sanctifying *truth* reveal?

What does God do regarding sin?

What is the ultimate purpose of *truth, salvation,* and *redemption*?

How does God punish sin?

How do we put on the new man?

How can we apply *this truth* to ourselves?

What are we to remember regarding the Twenty-third Psalm and the shepherd?

Chapter 13

SPEAKING THE TRUTH

Wherefore putting away lying, SPEAK EVERY MAN TRUTH WITH HIS NEIGHBOUR: *for we are members one of another.*

BE YE ANGRY, AND SIN NOT: *let not the sun go down upon your wrath:*

Neither give place (an opportunity) *to the devil.*

Let him that stole steal no more: but rather let him labour, working with his hands the thing which is good, that he may have to give to him that needeth.

Let no corrupt communication proceed out of your mouth, but that which is good to the use of edifying, that it may minister grace unto the hearers.

And grieve not the holy Spirit of God, whereby ye are sealed unto the day of redemption.

Let all bitterness, and wrath, and anger, and clamour, and evil speaking, be put away from you, with all malice:

And be ye kind one to another, tenderhearted, forgiving one another, even as God for Christ's sake (in Christ forgave) *hath forgiven you.*

BE *ye therefore followers of God, as dear children;*

And walk in love, as Christ also hath loved us, and hath given himself for us an offering and a sacrifice to God for a sweetsmelling savour (aroma) [Eph. 4:25–5:2].

What are we to remember as we continue to walk with Paul?

Why do we forget the incalculable wealth available in Christ?

What does it really mean to *put on the new man*?

Why does Paul want us to change holy teachings into holy conduct?

Why does Paul begin these teachings by addressing the subject of lying with respect to Christlike conduct?

What does Jesus say about lying and its source?

What are the unique characteristics of lying?

What causes lying?

What is included in the command to *SPEAK EVERY MAN TRUTH WITH HIS NEIGHBOR*?

What impact does lying have on true fellowship?

Chapter 14

ANGER—SINFUL OR RIGHTEOUS

> *Be ye angry, and sin not: let not the sun go down upon your wrath* [Eph. 4:26].

On whom are we to focus regarding Christlike conduct?

How is anger expressed?

How does anger negatively affect a person?

When do we sin in anger?

What offends God when we are angry?

What does the Apostle mean by *Be ye angry and sin not*?

How did Jesus express anger?

How is the wrath of God expressed?

What does Paul say in his letter to the Corinthians about anger?

What is meant by "Godly joy" and "Godly sorrow"?

What does the Apostle Paul mean by *Yea, what indignation*?

What is meant by the term *wrath* in *Let not the sun go down on your wrath*?

What happens when we are controlled by emotion?

Why does Paul say, *Neither give place to the devil*, as he discusses our dealing with anger?

What is the contrast to sinful anger and the bitter fruit it produces?

How are we to treat sin?

Why are we to cleanse ourselves of sinful anger?

Chapter 15

STEAL NO MORE, LABOR, AND GIVE TO THE NEEDY

> *Let him that stole steal no more: but rather let him labour, working with his hands the thing which is good, that he may have to give to him that needeth* [Eph. 4:28].

What commandment and motivation does Paul proclaim along with the prohibition to steal no more?

What does Scripture say about the person who steals?

What are the negative and positive injunctions regarding our character, conduct, and conversation?

What are the motivating factors for eliminating the negative and putting on the positive?

Why does the Apostle speak directly about stealing?

What do we need in order to grow and mature in our relationship with Christ?

Why does a person steal?

What does Scripture say we are to do regarding stealing?

Why does Paul say a person is to labor *that he may have to give to him that needeth*?

What is the rule governing true stewardship?

What does Paul's description of the Lord Jesus reveal to us?

Chapter 16

COMMUNICATING WITH BELIEVERS AND NON-BELIEVERS

> *Let no corrupt communication proceed out of your mouth, but that which is good to the use of edifying, that it may minister grace unto the hearers* [Eph. 4:29].

What are the fundamental truths contained in the Apostle John's testimony about the Lord Jesus?

What type person did Jesus select to be a faithful witness?

What is required to enjoy fellowship with the Lord Jesus?

Why are we to walk in the light?

What are the negative and positive injunctions for the command to *Let no corrupt communication proceed out of your mouth*?

What does Markus Barth say about speech?

What is our speech to be like as Christ's disciples?

What are the characteristics of corrupt communications?

What effect do corrupt communications have?

Why are we to use speech *That . . . is good to the use of edifying, as fits the occasion*?

What characteristics should be evident in our conversation as members of Christ's body?

Who is to be our example for good communications?

What words does Jesus use in His dealings with the people He encountered?

Chapter 17

GRIEVE NOT THE HOLY SPIRIT

And grieve not the holy Spirit of God, whereby ye are sealed unto the day of redemption [Eph. 4:30].

Why are we given the command, *Grieve not the Holy Spirit of God*?

What priority are we to establish in putting on the new man?

What is to be the basis of our thinking, conduct, behavior, and speech?

What does Paul tell us directly and forthrightly regarding the Holy Spirit?

What does the Holy Spirit enable men to do?

What are we, personally, to remember regarding the Holy Spirit?

What is stressed about the Holy Spirit in the New Testament?

What is a distinguishing mark on the sons of God?

Outline Questions 201

What should we remember about the Holy Spirit?

How do we grieve the Holy Spirit?

Why did Christ die on the Cross?

What happens when the Holy Spirit withholds His blessings?

Why has God established high and lofty standards for our walk in holiness?

Chapter 18

A WALK IN LOVE

> *Let all bitterness, and wrath, and anger, and clamour, and evil speaking, be put away from you, with all malice:*
> *And be ye kind one to another, tenderhearted, forgiving one another, even as God for Christ's sake hath forgiven you* [Eph. 4:31–32].

How does the Holy Spirit work?

How are we to walk in love?

Why does Jesus say we are to seek the weightier matters of life?

What does faith mean as used by Jesus?

What do John and Paul say regarding keeping God's commandments?

How is the Gospel of Christ to be received?

What did Paul realize regarding Christ's truth and love?

What does John say about love?

How are we to express our love for God and Christ?

What does Christ require of us?

How does Calvin describe love?

What negative injunctions does Paul present regarding love and our conduct?

What responsibility do we have regarding sins and sinful conditions?

What is required to progress properly as Christ's disciples?

What does Paul's positive commandment tell us to do?

Why are we to become kind, tenderhearted, and forgiving?

For what reasons did God bestow His love upon us?

Bibliography

Barth, Markus. Ephesians 1-3 and 4-6. Garden City, NY: Doubleday & Company, Inc., 1974.
Calvin, John. Calvin's New Testament Commentaries. Grand Rapids, MI: William. B. Eerdmans Publishing Company, 1959, 1960, 1961, 1963, 1965, 1972, 1973.
Calvin, John. Calvin's Sermons on The Epistle to the Ephesians. Carlisle, PA: The Banner of Truth Trust, 1973.
Calvin, John. Institutes of the Christian Religion. Philadelphia, PA: The Westminster Press.
Chambers, Oswald. My Utmost for His Highest. New York, NY: Dodd, Mead & Company.
Holy Bible. The King James Study Bible. Nashville, TN: Thomas Nelson, Inc., 1988.
Lloyd-Jones, Martyn. Darkness and Light. Grand Rapids, MI: Baker Book House, 1982.
Paxson, Ruth. The Wealth, Walk and Warfare of the Christian. London and Edinburgh: Oliphants, Ltd., 1941.
Presbyterian Hymnal. Louisville, KY: Westminster/John Knox Press, 1990.
Vine, W. E. Vine's Expository Dictionary of New Testament Words. McLean, VA: MacDonald Publishing Company.
Weber, Otto. Foundations of Dogmatics. Volumes 1 & 2. Grand Rapids, MI: William B. Eerdmans Publishing Company, 1981, 1983

Index of Scripture References
Volume 5

Genesis

1:1	35
3:1	72
17:1	97

Exodus

15:11	35
20:9	135

Leviticus

26:12	96

2 Kings

20:3	102

Job

31:1	83
31:7–8	83

Psalms

15:1–2	102
16:5	139
16:8–9	139
24:3–6	106
31:5	101
36:6	35
42:1–2	34
51:6	102
96:13	101
97:10–12	125
103:2–3	165
108:4	102
119:151	102

Proverbs

4:25	83
23:7	92

Isaiah

52:1	96
60:2	25

Jeremiah

2:13	34
5:1	102
6:15–21	36–37
17:9	74

Ezekiel

3:17–20	13

Hosea

4:6	35

Habakkuk

3:2	122

Matthew

5:13	49
5:14	49
5:16	9
6:21	139
6:24	128
10:20	151
12:34–37	142
13:12	4
18:22	126
18:35	126
19:17	33
22:36–37	118
22:37	159
22:39	119, 159
23:23	157
25:29	4

Mark

3:1–5	122
9:24	6

Luke

2:11	20
4:18	151
5:36–39	66
11:24	62
11:26	63
22:15	70

John

2:12–17	122–123
3:4–6	34
3:19	25
3:21	104
4:22–26	104
5:26	32
6:45	43
8:12	25
8:31–32	100, 101
8:43–44	116
8:44	72
9:25	15
10:10	151
13:17	4
13:34	159
14:6	57, 100, 119, 137
14:15	159
14:15–18	86–87
14:21	160
14:23	88
15:10	160
16:13	103, 115
17:3	33
17:14	48
17:17	103

Acts

2:4	151
2:42	41
4:7–8	57
4:10–12	56–57
4:20	45
9:1	85
9:13	85
9:16	86
9:17–18	85
9:20	85
9:31	143
16:14	54
20:20–21	41
20:21	43
20:25–27	12
20:27	13
20:34–35	134
26:18	25

Romans

1:16	47, 123
1:18	123
1:18–19	12, 13

6:6	64
6:11	107
6:12–13	140
6:16–18	105
6:19	90
7:15	7
7:19	114
8:5–8	91
8:9–11	152
8:13	83
12:19–21	127
13:12	82
13:14	82
15:8	102

1 Corinthians

1:26–29	26
1:30	105
1:31	26
2:10	30
2:10–11	53
2:14	91
2:16	28
3:1–2	146
3:16	109
4:1–2	135
4:12–13	134
6:9–10	130
6:19–20	152
7:6	14
8:1	144
9:27	83
10:23	144
14:4	143
14:17	144

2 Corinthians

3:13–16	23
3:16	24
4:3–6	24
4:4	25
5:17	131
5:17–19	61
6:1	94
6:3–4	94
6:4–5	94
6:6–7	94–95
6:8–10	95
6:16	49
6:17	96
6:17–18	96
6:18	108
7:1	96
7:8–11	123
7:10	124
11:3	72, 116
11:10	102
11:31	68
13:3	45

Galatians

2:5	102
2:14	6
3:1	115
5:19–21	153

Ephesians

1:1	5
1:4	154
1:13	151
2:1–2	91
2:2–3	16
2:4–7	16
2:10	80
2:11–13	3
2:15	60
2:19–20	5, 15
2:22	5
3:14	29
3:16	60
3:16–19	29
3:16–20	77

Ephesians - continued

4:1	52, 101, 156
4:4–6	111
4:12–13	112
4:16	28
4:17	11, 15, 20, 170, 172
4:17–18	3
4:17–19	1, 14, 21, 31, 168, 174
4:19	36
4:20	22, 39, 77
4:20–21	40, 50, 178
4:20–22	69–70, 148
4:20–24	176
4:21	46, 83, 139, 150
4:21–22	60
4:22	63, 77, 79, 83, 85, 103
4:22–24	58, 68, 76, 180, 182, 184
4:23	85, 86, 186
4:24	60, 77, 79, 83, 85, 93, 101, 103, 129–130, 148, 149, 150, 188, 190
4:25	111, 116, 119, 140, 145
4:25–26	148
4:25–31	130
4:25–5:2	130, 131, 192
4:26	79, 120, 145, 194
4:26–27	127, 128
4:27	120, 126
4:28	79, 129, 196
4:28–29	148
4:29	79, 137, 140, 143, 144, 198
4:30	148, 149, 150, 151, 153, 155, 163, 200
4:31	79, 140
4:31–32	156, 202
4:32	79, 165, 166
5:3	140
5:11	82

Philippians

1:27	63, 81
2:4–11	135–136
3:12–13	159

Colossians

1:5	115
3:1–2	112
3:9	118
3:9–10	65
3:11	65
3:12–13	66
3:14–16	66

1 Thessalonians

5:5	108
5:11	144

2 Thessalonians

2:10	103
2:12	103

1 Timothy

2:3–4	51
3:15	115
4:1–2	37
4:6	42

2 Timothy

1:6	107

Titus

1:1	114, 115
1:1–2	114
1:2	116
2:11	139
2:12	139

Hebrews

3:8	73
3:13	73
3:15	74
4:7	74
10:25	108

James

1:18	34
3:5–8	141

1 Peter

1:23	34
2:9–12	47–48
2:11–12	109
3:8–9	164
3:15	52

2 Peter

1:3	32
1:4	32
1:8	155
2:12–14	72
2:15–19	73
2:19–20	73

1 John

1:1	137
1:3	137
1:6	104
1:7	21, 69
2:4	116
2:7–8	157
2:10–11	157
3:14–15	160
3:17–18	158
5:4	20

3 John

1:3–4	104

Revelation

2:7	151

www.ingramcontent.com/pod-product-compliance
Lightning Source LLC
Chambersburg PA
CBHW070312230426
43663CB00011B/2104